Marketing
for
Beginners

The Key Concepts & Steps for Young Executives

BITTU KUMAR

V&S PUBLISHERS

Published by:

V&S PUBLISHERS

F-2/16, Ansari Road, Daryaganj, New Delhi-110002
011-23240026, 011-23240027 • *Fax:* 011-23240028
Email: info@vspublishers.com • *Website:* www.vspublishers.com

Branch : Hyderabad
5-1-707/1, Brij Bhawan (Beside Central Bank of India Lane)
Bank Street, Koti, Hyderabad - 500 095
040-24737290
E-mail: vspublishershyd@gmail.com

Follow us on:

For any assistance sms **VSPUB** to **56161**

All books available at **www.vspublishers.com**

© **Copyright:** *V&S PUBLISHERS*
ISBN 978-93-815885-7-4
Edition 2013

Printed at : Param Offseters, Okhla, New Delhi-110020

This Book is dedicated to

Nirankari Baba Hardev Singh Ji Maharaj

Publisher's Note

After a number of books on Career Management, **V&S Publishers** has come out with an absolutely novel and exlusive book for its readers, particularly the school and college going students aspiring to build a career in Marketing.

Marketing, as we all know is definitely one of the greatest arts as well as technique that starts right from preparing a product or delivering a service, identifying a customer, satisfying him or her with the product or service and retaining the customer for a life time by developing various marketing strategies and incentives from time to time. This book comprehensively explains all these and much more providing the details on all the basic fundamentals of Marketing and Marketing Management, such as: *Brand Strategy, Pricing, Sales Process and Management, Marketing Plans, Budgeting, Telemarketing, Online Advertisements, E-mail Marketing, etc.*

The idea behind publishing this book is to educate and enlighten the readers, especially the younger generation about what Marketing actually means, how broad and challenging the subject is, and what are its salient features, principles, objectives and prospects.

Basically, the book aims to satisfy and answer all the queries relating to the market, the market strategies, relationship between a buyer and a seller, customer satisfaction and retention, vendor selection, return on investments, etc. So, read on and enrich your knowledge about this vast and interesting subject of Marketing.

Contents

Publisher's Note _____ 5
Introduction _____ 9

1. Competitive Positioning_____ 11
2. Brand Strategy _____ 15
3. Distribution Channels _____ 19
4. Pricing _____ 25
5. Sales Process_____ 30
6. Marketing Campaigns _____ 34
7. Marketing Plan & Budget_____ 39
8. Naming _____ 43
9. Corporate Identity_____ 47
10. Messaging_____ 50
11. Sales Literature & Tools _____ 53
12. Websites _____ 56
13. Customer Relationship Management (CRM) _____ 61
14. Sales Management _____ 66
15. Business Development _____ 70
16. Customer Retention _____ 74
17. Telemarketing_____ 78
18. Trade Shows & Events _____ 83
19. E-mail Marketing_____ 88
20. Search Marketing_____ 93

21. Online Advertising _____ 97

22. Publicity _____ 101

23. Direct Mail _____ 105

24. Traditional Media _____ 109

25. Recruiting _____ 113

26. Vendor Selection _____ 117

27. Return on Investment (ROI)_____ 120

28. Customer Lifetime Value (CLV) _____ 124

29. Copywriting & Graphic Design _____ 128

Introduction

What is marketing? It's a broad, challenging and often misunderstood function. Ask several people to define it and you'll probably get very different answers:

- ❏ Some may say it's brochures, slogans and print ads in magazines.
- ❏ Others may be of the view that it's websites and e-mail campaigns.
- ❏ For few, it may be just communicating with customers.
- ❏ Some may be of the opinion that it's an MBA crunching numbers on band equity and market shares.

Yet marketing is much more than brochures, websites and numbers; *it's an investment that generates revenue, profit and opportunity for growth.*

Marketing is the process of developing and communicating value to your prospects and customers. Think about every step you take to sell service and manage your customers:

- ❏ Your knowledge of the market and your strategy to penetrate it
- ❏ The distribution channels you use to connect with your customers
- ❏ Your pricing strategy
- ❏ The messages you deliver to your market
- ❏ The look and feel of your marketing materials

The experience you deliver to your market and customers

The actions of your sales and service representatives

All of the planning, preparation, forecasting and measurement of your investments

Good marketing is essential for every company. It can make a company with a mediocre product successful, but poor marketing can send a good company out of business. Yet even Business-to-Business (B2B) marketing is often seen as a soft creative field instead of the engine that drives the company revenue.

Key concepts & steps

The Strategic Marketing Process organises 29 marketing subjects into three broad categories:

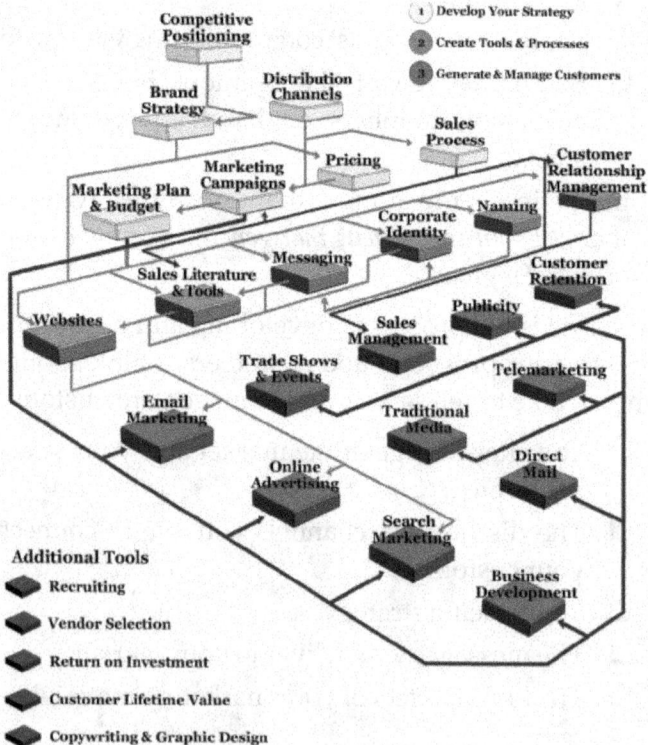

CHAPTER 1

Competitive Positioning

What sets your product, service and company apart from your competitors? What value do you provide and how is it different than the alternatives? Competitive positioning is about defining how you'll "differentiate" your offering and create value for your market. It's about carving out a spot in the competitive landscape and focussing your company to deliver on that strategy. A good strategy includes:

- ❑ Market profile: size, competitors, stage of growth
- ❑ Customer segments: groups of prospects with similar wants and needs
- ❑ Competitive analysis: strengths, weaknesses, opportunities and threats in the landscape
- ❑ Positioning strategy: how you'll position your offering to focus on opportunities in the market
- ❑ Value proposition: the type of value you'll deliver to the market

When your market clearly sees how your offering is different than that of your competition, it's easier to generate new prospects and guide them to buy. Without differentiation, it takes more time and money to show prospects why they should choose you; as a result, you often end up competing on price – a tough position to sustain over the long term.

One of the key elements of your positioning strategy is your value proposition. There are three essential types of value: operational excellence, product leadership and customer intimacy.

Cases in Market

Best Case	Neutral Case	Worst Case
You provide a one-of-a-kind product/service that your market needs and wants. You have a strong value proposition that differentiates you from your competitors; you communicate it consistently in everything you do. Your prospects respond because you're meeting their needs, and your company has found success in the market.	Your product is somewhat different and better than those of your competitors and you communicate that difference, though probably not as consistently as you should. Your prospects partially buy into the value you provide, but you don't win all of the deals that you could.	Your prospects see little difference between you and your competitors, so you're competing solely on price. You have to fight long and hard for every sale. It's very difficult to meet your Revenue and Profit goals.

Key concepts & steps

Before you begin

Your competitive positioning strategy is the foundation of your entire business – it's the first thing you should do if you're launching a new company or product. It's also important when you're expanding or looking for a new edge.

Profile your market

- ❑ Document the size of your market, major competitors and how they're positioned.
- ❑ Determine whether your market is in the introductory, growth, mature, or declining stage of its life. This "lifecycle stage" affects your entire marketing strategy.

Segment your market

- ❑ Understand the problems that your market faces. Talk with prospects and customers, or conduct research if you have the time, budget and opportunity. Uncover their true wants and needs – you'll learn a great deal about what you can deliver to solve their problems and beat your competitors.
- ❑ Group your prospects into "segments" that have similar problems and can use your product in similar ways. By grouping them into segments, you can efficiently market to each group.

Evaluate your competition

- ❑ List your competitors. Include any of your competitors that can solve your customers' problems, even if their solutions are much different than yours – they're still your competitors.
- ❑ Rate your own company and your direct competitors on operational efficiency (price), product leadership and customer intimacy. It's easy to think you're the best, so be as impartial as you can.

Stake a position

- ❑ Identify areas where your competition is vulnerable.
- ❑ Determine whether you can focus on those vulnerable areas – they are your major opportunities.
- ❑ Identify products/services you can offer to meet the true needs of your market in a new and better way.

Define your value proposition

- ❑ There are three core types of values that a company can deliver: operational efficiency (the lowest price), product leadership (the best product), and customer intimacy (the best solution and service).
- ❑ Determine which one you're best equipped to deliver; your decision is your "value proposition."

What's next?

Develop a brand strategy to help you communicate your positioning and value proposition every time you touch your market. Together, these strategies are the essential building blocks for your business.

CHAPTER 2

Brand Strategy

What is a brand? Is it a logo, a name or a slogan? Is it a graphic design or a colour scheme? Your brand is the entire experience your prospects and customers have with your company. It's what you stand for, a promise you make, and the personality you convey. And while it includes your logo, colour palette and slogan, those are only creative elements that convey your brand. Instead, your brand lives in every day-to-day interaction you have with your market. It is basically

- ❑ The images you convey
- ❑ The messages you deliver on your website, proposals and sales materials
- ❑ The way your employees interact with customers
- ❑ A customer's opinion of you versus your competition

Branding is crucial for products and services sold in huge consumer markets. It's also important in B2B because it helps you stand out from your competition. It brings your competitive position and value proposition to life. It positions you as a certain "something" in the mind of your prospects and customers. Your brand consistently and repeatedly tells your prospects and customers why they should buy from you. Think about successful consumer brands like *Disney*, *Tiffany* or *Starbucks*. You probably know what each brand represents. Now imagine that you're competing against one of these companies. If you want to capture significant market share, start with a strong and unique brand identity or you may not get far.

In your industry, there may or may not be a strong B2B brand. But when you put two companies up against each other, the one that represents something valuable will have an easier time reaching, engaging, closing and retaining customers. A strong brand strategy can be a big advantage.

Successful branding also creates "brand equity" – the amount of money that customers are willing to pay just because it's your brand. In addition to generating revenue, brand equity makes your company itself more valuable over the long term.

By defining your brand strategy and using it in every inter-action with your market, you strengthen your messages and relationships.

Best Case	Neutral Case	Worst Case
Prospects and customers know exactly what you deliver. It's easy to begin dialogue with new prospects because they quickly understand what you stand for. You close deals more quickly because your prospects' experience with you and support everything you say. You can charge a premium because your market knows why you're better and is willing to pay for it.	The market may not have a consistent view or impression of your product and company, but in general you think it's positive. You haven't thought a lot about branding because it doesn't necessarily seem relevant, but you admit that you can do a better job of communicating consistently with the market. You're not helping yourself but you're not hurting yourself either.	You don't have a brand strategy and it shows. It's more difficult to communicate with prospects and convince them to buy. They don't have an impression of your product or why it's better. What you do, what you say and how you say it, may contradict each other and confuse your prospects. Competitors who communicate more strongly have a better shot at talking with and closing your prospective customers.

Key concepts & steps

Before you begin

Before working on your brand strategy, make sure you've identified your competitive position – your brand strategy will bring it to life.

If you have a brand strategy, make sure it's as effective as possible

❏ Poll your customers, employees and vendors. Are their impressions consistent with your strategy? If not, work on the elements you can improve.

Develop your brand strategy around emotional benefits

❏ List the features and benefits of your product/service. A feature is an attribute – a colour, a configuration; a benefit is what that feature does for the customer.

❏ Determine which benefits are most important to each of your customer segments.

❏ Identify which benefits are emotional – the most powerful brand strategies tap into emotions, even among the business buyers.

❏ Look at the emotional benefits and boil them down to one thing that your customers should think of when they think of you. That's what your brand should represent.

Define your brand

❏ Think of your brand as a person with a distinct personality. Describe him or her, then convey these traits in everything you do and create.

❏ Write positioning statements and a story about your brand; use them throughout your company materials.

Choose colours, fonts and other visual elements that match your personality.

Determine how your employees will interact with prospects and customers to convey the personality and make sure your brand "lives" within your company.

What's next?

Together with your competitive positioning strategy, your brand strategy is the essence of what you represent. A great brand strategy helps you to communicate more effectively with your market, so follow it in every interaction you have with your prospects and customers.

For example, you'll communicate your brand strategy through your pricing strategy, name and corporate identity, messages, literature and website. It may also drive the need to implement a better Cutormer Relationship Management (CRM) system to manage customer relationships.

CHAPTER 3

Distribution Channels

How do you sell to your end-users? Do you use a direct sales team, resellers, a catalogue or a website? Distribution channels are the pathways that companies use to sell their products to end-users. B2B companies can sell through a single channel or through multiple channels that may include:

❏ Direct/Sales team: One or more sales teams that you employ directly. You may use multiple teams that specialise in different products or customer segments.

❏ Direct/Internet: Selling through your own e-commerce website.

❏ Direct/Catalogue: Selling through your own catalogue.

❏ Wholesaler/Distributor: A company that buys products in bulk from many manufacturers and then resells smaller volumes to the resellers or retailers.

❏ Value-added Reseller (VAR): A VAR works with end-users to provide customer solutions that may include multiple products and services from different manufacturers.

❏ Consultant: A consultant develops relationships with companies and provides either specific or very broad services; they may recommend a manufacturer's product or simply purchase it to deliver a solution for the customer.

❑ Dealer: A company or person who buys inventory from either a manufacturer or distributor, and then re-sells to an end-user.

❑ Retail: Retailers sell directly to the end-users via a physical store, website or catalogue.

❑ Sales agent/Manufacturer's representative: You can outsource your sales function to a company that sells different manufacturers' products to a group of similar customers in a specific territory.

❑ Distribution is one of the classic "4 Ps" of marketing (product, promotion, price, placement a.k.a. distribution). It's a key element in your entire marketing strategy — it helps you to expand your reach and grow your revenue.

Direct To End-Users	Sell Through A Dealer Network	Sell Through A VAR (Value-Added Reseller)
You have a sales team that sells directly to the Fortune 100 companies. You have a second product line for small businesses. Instead of using your sales team, you sell this line directly to end-users through your website and marketing campaigns. You have two markets and two distribution channels.	You sell a product through a geographical network of dealers who sell to end-users in their areas. The dealers may service the product as well. Your dealers are essentially your customers, and you have a strong program to train and support them with marketing campaigns and materials.	You sell a product to a company who bundles it with services or other products and resells it. That company is called a Value Added Reseller (VAR) because it adds value to your product. A VAR may work with an end-user to determine the right products and configurations, and then implement a system that includes your product.

To create a good distribution program, focus on the needs of your end-users.

❑ If they need personalised service, you can utilise a local dealer network or reseller program to provide that service.

❑ If your users prefer to buy online, you can create an e-commerce website and fulfilment system, and sell directly; you can also sell to another online retailer or a distributor to offer your product on their own sites.

❑ You can build your own specialised sales team to prospect and close deals directly with customers.

Wholesalers, resellers, retailers, consultants and agents already have resources and relationships to quickly bring your product to market. If you sell through these groups instead of (or in addition to) selling directly, treat the entire channel as a group of customers – and they are, since they are buying your product and reselling it. Understand their needs and deliver strong marketing programs; you'll maximise everyone's revenue in the process.

Best Case	Neutral Case	Worst Case
You've used one or more distribution channels to grow your revenue and market share more quickly than you would have otherwise. Your end-users get the information and service they need before and after the sale. If you reach your end-user through wholesalers, VARs or other channel partners, you've created many successful marketing programs to drive revenue through your channel and you're committed to their success.	You're using one or more distribution channels with average success. You may not have as many channel partners as you'd like, but your current system is working moderately well. You devote resources to the program, but you wonder whether you'd be better off building an alternative distribution method – one that could help you grow more aggressively than you are now. You probably aren't hitting your revenue goals because your distribution strategy is in trouble. With your current system, you may not be effectively reaching your end-users;	You probably aren't hitting your revenue goals because your distribution strategy is in trouble. With your current system, you may not be effectively reaching your end-users; your prospects probably aren't getting the information and service they need to buy your product. Your current system may also be difficult to manage. For example, channel members may not sell at your suggested price; they don't follow up on leads you deliver; they don't

Table Contd......

Best Case	Neutral Case	Worst Case
	your prospects probably aren't getting the information and service they need to buy your product. Your current system may also be difficult to manage. For example, channel members may not sell at your suggested price; they don't follow up.	service the product very well and you're taking calls from angry Customers.

Key concepts & steps

Before you begin

You can evaluate a new distribution channel or improve your channel marketing / management at any time. It's especially important to think about distribution when you're going after a new customer segment, releasing a new product, or looking for ways to aggressively grow your business.

Evaluate how your end-users need to buy

Your distribution strategy should deliver the information and service your prospects need. For each customer segment, consider the following:

❑ How and where they prefer to buy

❑ Whether they need personalised education and training

❑ Whether they need additional products or services to be used alongside yours

❑ Whether your product needs to be customised or installed

❑ Whether your product needs to be serviced

Match end-user needs to a distribution strategy

❑ If your end-users need a great deal of information and service, your company can deliver it directly through a sales force. You can also build a channel of qualified resellers, consultants or resellers. The size of the market and your price will probably dictate which scenario is best.

❏ If the buying process is fairly straightforward, you can sell directly via a website/catalog or perhaps, through a wholesale/retail structure. You may also use an inbound telemarketing group or a field sales team.

❏ If you need complete control over your product's delivery and service, adding a channel probably isn't right for you.

Identify natural partners

❏ If you want to grow beyond the direct model, look for companies that have relationships with your end-users.

❏ If consultants, wholesalers or retailers already reach your customer base, they're called natural partners.

Build your channel

If you're setting up a distribution channel with one or more partners, treat it as a sales process:

❏ Approach the potential channel partner and "sell" the value of the partnership.

❏ Establish goals, service requirements and reporting requirements.

❏ Deliver inventory (if necessary) and sales/support materials.

❏ Train the partner.

❏ Run promotions and programs to support the partner and help them increase sales.

Minimise pricing conflicts

If you use multiple channels, carefully map out the price for each step in your channel and include a fair profit for each type of partner. Then compare the price that the end-user will pay; if a customer can buy from one channel at a lower price than another, your partners will rightfully have concerns. Pricing conflict is common, but it can jeopardise your entire strategy, so do your best to map out the price at each step and develop the best solution possible.

Drive revenue through the channel

Service your channel partners as you'd service your best customers and work with them to drive revenue. For example, provide them with marketing funds or materials to promote your products; run campaigns to generate leads and forward them to your partners.

What's next?

As you're creating a new channel, you'll need a pricing strategy and sales process. When your channel is up and running, you can start launching marketing campaigns to channel partners and end-users.

CHAPTER 4

Pricing

Price is one of the classic "4 Ps" of marketing (product, **price**, place, promotion). Yet in many B2B companies, marketers aren't necessarily involved in pricing strategy.

Pricing is a complex subject – there are many factors to consider, both short and long-term. For example, your prices need to

- ❏ Reflect the value you provide versus your competitors
- ❏ Consider what the market will truly pay for your offering
- ❏ Enable you to reach your revenue and market share goals
- ❏ Maximise your profits

When you offer a truly unique product or service with little direct competition, it can be challenging to establish your price. Put together a strong strategy and competitive analysis so that you can see:

- ❏ What your prospects might pay for other solutions to their problems
- ❏ Where your price should fall in relation to theirs

When your price, value proposition and competitive position are aligned, you're in the best situation to maximise

revenue and profits. For example, here are three scenarios that show the relationship between these elements.

Highest Price	Average Price	Lowest Price
Company A is one of the best consulting firms in the world. Their consultants come from top schools, and they work with Fortune 100 clients to implement Complex, large-scale projects. Company A's value proposition is product leadership. Their clients are buying the best expertise they can find, and they're less sensitive to price because they care most about getting the top talents. Therefore, Company A's services can be priced as high as or higher than their competitors.	Like Company A, Company B's value proposition is product leadership, but their secondary value prop is Price. There's a lot of competition and their product is only slightly better than the alternatives. Company B's messages focus on product Leadership with a secondary focus on price. They regularly review the market, run promotions, and adjust prices to maintain their competitive position.The company is also working to develop a premium product that can warrant a higher price.	The market cares most about price because the product is viewed as a commodity. Company C focusses on finding new ways to lower costs and pass savings on to customers. Their value proposition is operational efficiency and they consistently deliver the same product at a better price. Company C regularly evaluates their competitors' prices to make sure they're delivering on their promise. If a competitor runs a promotion, Company C counters with a better one.

What would happen if these companies used a different pricing strategy?

Highest Price	Average Price	Lowest Price
By dropping their hourly rate, Company A gains more clients. They hire more consultants, but since they're charging less per hour, they can't afford the same top-tier talent.	If Company B charges a premium price for an average product, they'll have a very difficult time generating interest in their product.	If Company C's prices rise in relation to those of their competitors, their sales will plummet – their market is shopping on price, not factors like product leadership or customer intimacy.

Table Contd......

Highest Price	Average Price	Lowest Price
Company A is putting their "prestige" brand in jeopardy. However, if there isn't a strong market for prestige, this strategy may be the best one for the company in the long term.	Yet Company B may be able to implement a small price increase to raise revenue and profits; it depends how much more its customers are willing to spend. By analysing price sensitivity and testing different prices, they can evaluate the strength and potential of this new strategy.	If Company C cannot maintain its operational efficiency and cost leadership, it will need to develop new products or markets for its existing product.

Do you see your company in one of these scenarios?

Best Case	Neutral Case	Worst Case
Your price completely supports your value proposition, enabling you to maximise your revenue and profit.	You don't necessarily have a pricing strategy but you're probably in the right range. You enter a moderate number of price negotiations and you win some, lose some. You wonder whether you could increase revenue and profit with either a price increase or decrease.	Your price is misaligned with your value proposition and what your market is willing to pay. Your prospects and customers are constantly fighting with you on price, and it takes its toll on your team. You often have to discount heavily to make a sale.

Key concepts & steps

Before you begin

It's best to create your **brand strategy** and identify your **distribution channels** before you develop your pricing strategy. By doing so, you'll ensure that your pricing reflects your value proposition and reinforces your brand; you can also minimise pricing conflicts with your channel partners.

Match your pricing strategy to your value proposition

Your price sends a strong message to your market – it needs to be consistent with the value you're delivering.

❑ If your value proposition is operational efficiency, then your price needs to be extremely competitive.

❑ If your value proposition is product leadership or customer intimacy, a low price sends the wrong message. After all, if a luxury item isn't expensive, is it really a luxury?

Understand your cost structure and profitability goals

Companies calculate these costs differently, so verify the exact calculations your company uses for the following:

❑ Cost of Goods Sold (COGS): the cost to physically produce a product or service

❑ Gross profit: the difference between the revenue you earn on a product and the cost to physically produce it in addition, understand how much profit the company needs to generate. You'll be far more effective when considering the discount promotions – you'll know exactly how low you can go and still be profitable.

Analyse your competitors' prices

Look at a wide variety of direct and indirect competitors to gauge where your price falls. If your value proposition is operational efficiency, evaluate your competitors on a regular basis to ensure that you're continually competitive.

Determine price sensitivity

❑ A higher price typically means lower volume. Yet you may generate more total revenue and/or profit with fewer units at the higher price; it depends on how sensitive your customers are to price fluctuations. If they're extremely sensitive, you may be better off at a much lower price with substantially greater volume. Estimate how sensitive your customers are to

price and volume combination. More importantly, you can estimate how a price change can impact your revenue.

What's next?

Once you've finalised your pricing strategy, you can plan and launch your marketing campaigns.

CHAPTER 5

Sales Process

How do prospects buy your product or service? Does a single decision-maker find a product and multiple departments involved in the decision, each with its own needs?

A sales process is a defined series of steps you follow as you guide prospects from initial contact to purchase. It begins when you first identify a new prospect:

Step 1	Step 2	Step 3	Step 4	Step 5
A prospect responds to a campaign and requests information	A sales rep calls the prospect to explain your product	In-person meeting & product demo	Your team submits a proposal	Prospect signs an agreement and makes the first payment

A documented sales process is a flowchart that explains:

- ❑ Each distinct step a prospect takes
- ❑ Knowledge the prospect needs to move to the next step
- ❑ Literature and tools you can provide to help the prospect move forward
- ❑ Length of time a prospect needs at each step
- ❑ Conversion rates: the percentage of prospects who move from one step to the next

With a documented sales process, you have a powerful tool that enables you to:

❑ Sell more efficiently

❑ Generate more accurate sales and revenue reports

❑ Estimate the revenue and Return on Investment (ROI) of your marketing campaigns

❑ See which stages take the most time and find ways to move prospects forward

❑ Create better literature and tools

❑ Improve your campaigns

❑ Minimise the amount of time your reps spend on estimates and forecasts

Do you see your company in one of these scenarios?

Best Case	Neutral Case	Worst Case
You have a well-designed process that measures the number of prospects you have at each stage, how long they stay in each stage, and the revenue your entire pipeline represents. You deliver the right amount of information prospects need at each step, which helps them make decisions more quickly and move to the next stage. You use your sales process to create more successful marketing campaigns because you can predict how many leads will become customers and what those leads will be worth to your company.	You may or may not have a defined sales process. You generally follow the same steps to close a customer, but there's a big variance in the amount of time it takes to close. In fact, even your strongest reps have trouble closing certain types of prospects. Your forecasts are probably all manual and generally accurate, but you wish you had a thorough snapshot to show exactly how many accounts are at a certain stage and what you need to do to close.	You don't have a process or use one that doesn't match how prospects want to buy. You deliver all of the information about your product but then seem to lose control of the prospect. Some prospects end up buying, but you don't know why the others don't. It's a constant battle to figure out how many real prospects you have and what they're worth. Your sales team often spends valuable time creating manual reports instead of selling, which further hurts your revenue.

Key concepts & steps

Before you begin

If you don't have a defined sales process, it's a valuable investment that can improve your entire sales and marketing program. Create processes for each distribution channel, product and/or customer segment.

Determine how your prospects buy

List the steps you think prospects logically take from the time they recognise a problem to the time they buy. Talk with customers or ask your sales representatives for more insight. Figure out what steps they take, what they need to know and how you can deliver that information most effectively.

Create your process

For each step your prospects need to take, list

- ❑ What the prospect needs to learn
- ❑ Literature and tools you can provide to help the prospect move forward
- ❑ The length of time a prospect needs at the step
- ❑ The percentage of prospects who move from each step to the next (your "conversion rate")

Project campaign results & revenue

When you have a sales process with conversion rates, you can generate solid pipeline and revenue reports. For example, if you have 50 prospects at the presentation stage, your process may show that 20 percent will become customers. That means those 50 prospects should deliver 10 new customers. Your process will also tell you when that should happen and how much revenue those prospects represent.

You can use a similar calculation to project results from new marketing campaigns. For example, if a campaign should produce 100 qualified leads, you can estimate the number of meetings, presentations, and new customers the campaign will generate.

Improve your process to maximise revenue:

When you have a defined process, it's easier to test ideas for improving results. For example, you can

Identify spots where prospects get "stuck" in the process and try new materials or messages to help them move forward

Measure how well different representatives convert at each step and help those that aren't doing as well

See how leads from different marketing campaigns convert and improve your campaigns

Create campaigns to "recycle" leads that fall out of the process at various spots

What's next?

After you've documented your sales process, develop the **literature and tools** you'll need to guide your prospects through each step. Add your process to your **customer relationship management** (CRM) software so that each account is assigned to a stage at all times. Then you can run reports and measure your progress and improve your **sales management**.

You'll also use your sales process to measure the success of **marketing campaigns**. For example: for a specific campaign, you can see how many leads entered the process and made it to each step.

Basically, a sales process is a method to turn your **prospects** into **customers**.

CHAPTER 6

Marketing Campaigns

In many B2B companies, a sales team is the primary method for reaching out to the market. Salespeople call prospects and customers, but they can only do so much in a day. Marketing campaigns can dramatically increase your reach.

Generate New Leads	Drive Existing Prospects To Your Trade Show Booth & VIP Reception	Hit Your Market With A Special Offer
1. Use search to generate traffic to your website. 2. Prospect requests information via e-mail. 3. E-mail the requested information. 4. Call the prospect; qualify the prospect further and determine next steps.	1. Mail a postcard to attendees 3 weeks before the show; invite them to your booth with an intriguing incentive. 2. Mail a special invite to key prospects and customers for a VIP reception. Ask them to RSVP by phone, e-mail or URL. 3. Call key prospects and customers as a second effort.	1. Run banner ads on industry websites and targeted e-mail newsletters. 2. Send out a special e-mail to your house list. 3. Create an intriguing story and tie it to your offer. Write a search-optimised press release and post on your site. Also distribute releases and pitch to a key industry reporter.

Table Contd......

Generate New Leads	Drive Existing Prospects To Your Trade Show Booth & VIP Reception	Hit Your Market With A Special Offer
	4. Send an e-mail to all confirmed atten-dees about 3 days before the event. 5. E-mail the non-respondents one last time.	4. Run a series of paid search ads.

In B2B, it's always best to start with your company's annual goals and develop campaigns to meet those numbers. For example, when you know how many new customers you need, you can calculate how many leads you'll need, and then design campaigns to generate those leads throughout the year.

With solid planning, a jolt of creativity and focus on measurement, you'll be in a strong position for success.

Best Case	Neutral Case	Worst Case
You plan and execute your campaigns to hit specific goals. You don't always hit them, but you test and improve different elements; the Return On Investment (ROI) on your overall budget is above your goal. You focus on an offer and call-to-action, and you touch your prospects several times and follow up when appropriate. You recognise the challenges in measuring results, but you do what you can; it helps you improve the next time around.	Your campaigns aren't the most creative or the splashiest, but you've hit many of your marketing goals. You don't test but your response rate is fine. Yet when you're faced with ambitious annual goals, you have problems gaining budget approval. Since you stick with the same campaigns year after year, it's also difficult to figure out how to generate additional leads.	Your marketing programs tend to be reactive -- suddenly you're low on leads or falling short of your goals and you launch a campaign to fix the problem. Since your programs don't seem to work, it's difficult to gain budget approval for future campaigns that could be more well-planned and executed. It's a vicious cycle and you don't know how to get out of it.

Key concepts & steps

Before you begin

Your **brand** and **pricing** strategies play a significant role in your marketing efforts, so nail down those strategies before launching any major campaigns. If you sell through **multiple distribution channels**, don't forget to create campaigns for each. You'll also refer to your **sales process** to estimate the revenue and the ROI for each campaign.

Quantify your goals

❑ Plan your campaigns to meet your annual revenue and volume goals. For example, if you're trying to generate 100 new customers, figure out how many leads you'll need and when you'll need them.

❑ Think about how you'll use different media. For example, your sales team may be able to generate 30 percent of your leads through prospecting; the rest may come from telemarketing, e-mail, direct mail, search marketing, webinars, trade shows and more.

Generate campaign, ideas and strategies

❑ Identify all of the business goals that will need marketing support. You may need campaigns to generate and nurture prospects, sell direct or through a channel, or market to existing customers.

❑ Evaluate ideas and options: traditional sales activities, internet marketing, telemarketing, direct mail, e-mail, publicity and more.

Target your audience

With more specific targeting, you can speak more directly to the prospect and raise your response rates in the process.

Deliver one or two key messages and your call-to-action

❑ If you include every detail about your product and company, it's easy for prospects to become overwhelmed. Just move a prospect one step at a time.

❑ Be creative -- your market is bombarded with messages daily, so grab their attention and engage them.

Plan to measure

❑ When you measure your campaigns, it's easier to gain budget approval the next time around. You'll also know exactly which programs produce the highest return.

❑ Establish how you'll measure each campaign. If there are variables you can't measure, decide how you will account for those results.

❑ Identify how you'll capture the data you'll need – unique phone numbers, unique URLs, etc.

Plan your fulfilment

❑ Your fulfilment processes can help or hurt your close rate, so make sure you outline your requirements.

❑ For example, if you're running a campaign where prospects request a software demo and it doesn't arrive for a week, your prospects may lose interest.

Continually test and improve

❑ Even on a small campaign, you can evaluate your ad, copy, list or other factors before you spend your entire budget.

❑ Choose a subset of your list or two versions of an ad; test them in small quantities and choose the best one for rollout. Then you can test a second variable against the winner in the first test.

Keep the testing cycle going and track your results over time. You'll improve your response rates and return on investment.

What's next?

Include your major campaigns in your annual **marketing plan and budget**, then implement your plans and strategies throughout the year: **e-mail marketing, business development, trade shows, publicity, online advertising, customer retention** and more.

CHAPTER 7

Marketing Plan & Budget

Most businesspeople agree that good planning is essential for success. Even so, it's surprising that many companies don't create a thorough plan to generate and manage their customers.

A marketing plan is a detailed roadmap that outlines all your marketing strategies, tactics, activities, costs and projected results over a period of time. The plan keeps your entire team focussed on specific goals – it's a critical resource for your entire company.

A good marketing plan typically includes:

- ❑ Financial goals
- ❑ Positioning strategy
- ❑ Brand strategy
- ❑ Product/service overview
- ❑ Detailed goals by product, distribution channels and/or customer segments
- ❑ Sales plan
- ❑ Major marketing campaigns
- ❑ Detailed budget
- ❑ Dates to review progress

It takes time to develop a solid plan, but it's important because it ties all of your activities to tangible goals. It's also a great opportunity to focus on the future, generate new ideas, and inspire your team. Even a simple plan is better than none, but when you invest more effort upfront, you'll have a better roadmap towards your goals.

Best Case	Neutral Case	Worst Case
Your marketing plan is a detailed roadmap to meet your goals. You recognise that the time you invest to create a solid plan is perhaps the best time you'll invest all year – it helps you work through new strategies, issues, ideas and numbers. When it's done, your team focusses on executing the plan and measuring your progress all the year long. As a result, you've been able to hit your goals, grow your business, and enjoy the journey.	You're incredibly busy, so it's difficult to invest the time in a detailed marketing plan. Instead, you develop a basic plan that's based on last year's version. You include general revenue goals, general sales strategies, and basic campaigns; you stick with proven techniques. Budgets are based on last year's numbers. You could be more ambitious with your revenue goals if your company was willing to try new things, but, each year you stick your success with the same tried-and-true strategies.	You don't typically create a marketing plan. You have a budget, but the numbers are haphazard. Things change so quickly – why spend the time? You take a similar approach with the strategies that should drive a marketing plan. You probably don't have a positioning or brand strategy; you're missing out on distribution channels or partnerships; your campaigns are ineffective and you may not invest in customer retention.

Key concepts & steps

Before you begin

A marketing plan should address all of your strategies, tactics and budget, so you'll need to review your **brand strategy, pricing strategy and distribution channels** beforehand. You'll also outline your major **marketing campaigns** for the year since they'll be in your budget.

Set your annual goals

Build your entire marketing plan to achieve the goals that you define:

- ❑ Quantitative (numeric) goals, such as total revenue, profit, number of customers, units sold, and breakdowns by product or channel as needed.
- ❑ Strategic goals -- for example, you may want to expand into a new market with a new distribution channel, or you may need to reposition your brand to reflect a change in your business.

Highlight your competitive position, value proposition and brand strategy

- ❑ Your positioning strategy defines how you'll differentiate your offering from your competitors.
- ❑ Your value proposition defines the primary value you deliver: operational efficiency, product leadership or customer intimacy.
- ❑ Your brand strategy defines what you stand for and how you'll communicate with the market.

Outline any plans for your products & services

If you need to do anything to strengthen your product line and better deliver on your value proposition, address those issues in your plan.

Develop your tactical sales plan

- ❑ The number of sales representatives you'll need and the markets they'll target
- ❑ Whether you'll need to hire, train, or develop new compensation plans
- ❑ Top priority markets, industries or customer segments; if you have a list of key prospects, include them
- ❑ Your plan for managing current customers
- ❑ Plans for launching any new distribution channels and driving revenue through existing channels

Outline your major marketing campaigns

You don't need to list every campaign -- just outline your major promotional plans for the year. You'll need to set your budget too, so the more planning you do now, the better. Your plans should include:

The top three campaigns you'll run to generate leads, nurture customers, close, and/or market to existing customers

The media you'll use (for example, e-mail, online, print, telemarketing, trade shows, publicity, etc.)

example, a new website, an e-mail service provider, a new piece of software

Your Return On Investment (ROI) and other financial goals

Develop a budget

Budgeting can be a difficult process. Many companies just estimate or base their budget on last year.

An estimate is better than nothing, but if you've defined your major campaigns and needs, you can develop better numbers.

You can also use your ROI to determine the appropriate total budget for your marketing efforts.

Revisit your plan regularly

The planning process itself is incredibly valuable, but if you don't review the plan regularly, it's easy to lose focus. Continually revisit the plan and measure your progress.

What's next?

When you've finished your plan, it's time to execute. You may need to create new messages, literature, website or other tools and processes for your campaigns, but after that, focus on generating and managing your customers.

CHAPTER 8

Naming

How important is the name of your product, service or company? It depends on your industry, the amount of time you've been in business, your competitors and how you want to position yourself in the market.

Your name is an extension of your brand, and it can reinforce the value you provide or distance you from it. When you're developing a name, you have a number of options:

- ❑ Use the founder or inventor's name (Hewlett-Packard)
- ❑ Describe what you do (Southwest Airlines)
- ❑ Describe an experience or image (Sprint)
- ❑ Take a word out of context (Apple)
- ❑ Make up a word (Google)

It's important to decide what your name should mean and represent. For example, if you're running a company that provides naming services, your name is a sample of your work – it should be great, right?

Here are some companies famous for providing naming services. The ABC Namebank, Addis Creson, Addison, Baer Design Group, etc.

Best Case	Neutral Case	Worst Case
A great name can create buzz, position you as a true leader and innovator, and reinforce your value proposition in a word or two. That's powerful. It can convey a culture, a position, and differentiate the company from the rest of the market.	You look and sound like everybody else. You've missed an opportunity to convey an important message, but at least you're not hurting yourself.	A poor name can neutralise or even negate the work you do to build a position in the market. You may have trouble generating interest in your company and spend more time and money educating the market about your value. A poor name can also limit your opportunities if you expand into other markets.

Key concepts & steps

Before you begin

Since your name is an extension of your brand, it's important to develop your brand strategy before you start the naming process.

Do you need to hire someone?

With a good process and strategy, you can probably develop a good name on your own. However, you may not have the resources or desire to handle the project internally. While it's no guarantee that a firm or consultant will develop a better name, they may do it more quickly and objectively.

There are a number of factors to consider, including:

- ❑ The stakes: If you're investing a lot of money launching a new product to a major market with established competition, the stakes are high.
- ❑ Your confidence in your team's creative firepower or objectivity.
- ❑ The amount of time and energy you have to devote to the project.

❑ Whether you can afford to bring in an outside resource.

Develop a strategy

❑ Determine what your name needs to accomplish.

❑ Decide how it will work with the existing product or service names (if applicable).

❑ Determine what kind of name to develop – descriptive, invented, founder's name, etc.

❑ Develop objective criteria to evaluate the names you generate.

Generate plenty of potential names

If you're competing beyond your local area, you may find that many of your potential names (or URLs) are already taken, so you'll need a long list. Invite a variety of people for a brainstorming session; plan it well and capture every idea for further evaluation.

Evaluate the list against your criteria

Your goal is to objectively find the name that meets y o u r criteria, so be careful about asking friends and family whether they "like" a name. For example, a name that raises eyebrows may do so because it's different – and it may be the most memorable and powerful one in the bunch.

❑ Also test the name to make sure it sounds good over the phone (for example, when a sales representative calls a prospect)

❑ Won't be constantly mispronounced or misspelled, which defeats the purpose of a name

❑ Isn't confusing

❑ Conveys what you need it to convey

❑ Has a URL that works with it

Protect your name: It's important to protect your name to the appropriate degree. If you choose a name that infringes on another company's copyright, you could receive a cease-and-desist letter and have to go to court and/or change your name after months or even years of use. By protecting your name, you also gain the ability to prevent future competitors from using it.

What's next?

After you select a new name, you can create your logo and **corporate identity**, then begin creating the **messages** to use throughout your sales materials and marketing efforts.

CHAPTER 9

Corporate Identity

When was the last time someone gave you a fantastic business card? Did you turn it over and look at it closely? Did you comment on it? And did you generate some sort of impression of that person and company?

Corporate identity is an extension of your brand and includes everything with your logo or contact information:

- ❑ Business cards
- ❑ Envelopes
- ❑ Letterhead
- ❑ Mailing labels
- ❑ E-mail templates and signatures
- ❑ Fax covers
- ❑ Proposal/quote templates
- ❑ Invoices/statements
- ❑ Memos
- ❑ Signage
- ❑ Promotional items

Many companies spend time and money on things like business cards yet overlook proposal templates, invoices and e-mail signatures that prospects see more frequently. For example, when an employee customises an e-mail template with unusual designs or fonts, it can contradict an expensive and serious business card – and convey a far different impression to the customer. Each element in your identity should use the same fonts, colours, layout, etc. The design itself may not be incredibly important unless you're in a creative field, but consistency and professionalism make an impression. In many cases, it may be a first impression, so why not make a good one?

Best Case	Neutral Case	Worst Case
Every touch with your prospects and customers is consistent and professional. They see a simple, effective design that strengthens your messages.	Some of your identity is great and other things, like invoices or shipping labels, don't match up. Prospects and customers probably notice, but you don't think it's a problem.	Your prospects and customers see a mishmash of poorly-produced identity. They may wonder how you can deliver the product or service you're selling if you can't produce a professional-looking document.

Before you begin

Naturally you need a **name** before you can create your corporate identity. You should also develop a **brand strategy** since your identity should support it and help bring it to life.

If you're already in business, does all of your identity reflect your brand?

Check everything from invoices and shipping labels to e-mail signatures. Make sure your logo is used correctly. Sometimes, they get accidentally resized) and that all of your materials are consistent with your value proposition and brand strategy. For example, if you're focussing on innovative, expensive new products, but you have flimsy business cards, you're not reinforcing your value.

Create professional, consistent templates for every touch with your market

Use a consistent style for everything your company sends out. It make take only ten minutes to create a better template, and that template may be seen by hundreds or thousands of prospects and customers over time.

Keep inventory

Templates can be altered or misplaced. So make sure that your team knows how to use them and check them regularly.

What's next?

Once you've finished with your identity, the typical next step is to focus on your **sales literature** and your **website**.

Chapter 10

Messaging

How do you respond when someone asks, "What does your company do?" Do all your team members answer the same way? Is your response compelling so that the listener wants to learn more, or do you sound like everyone else? **'Messages' are written and verbal statements that quickly describe what you do and how you're different.** They're used throughout your interactions with your market:

The "elevator pitch" – the 30-second response to "what do you do?" Sales and marketing materials – sales literature, websites, presentations and campaigns all use messages of various lengths. The introductory statement in a phone call, press releases – the blurb at the bottom of the release that explains what your company does and slogans – Your mission statement.

Good messages take your competitive positioning and brand strategy to the next level. They hone in on what's important to your market and communicate it consistently and effectively.

Best Case	Neutral Case	Worst Case
By carefully crafting your messages, you can strengthen your value proposition, your brand and the reasons your prospects should buy. It's easy to communicate your value. The market "gets it" very quickly, speeding up the sales process.	Ho-hum messages don't help you stand out, but as long as they're not inaccurate or poorly written, they probably won't hurt. You just miss out on the opportunity to strengthen your position.	Without consistent messages, individual team members do their own authoring and the results are rarely good, let alone consistent. Poor messages confuse the market and can contradict the other strategies you've worked hard to implement.

Before you begin

Before you start writing, define your **brand strategy** – it will help you identify what your messages should convey. If you need messages for a **marketing campaign** or program from your **marketing plan**, plan them out so you'll know exactly what kind of messages you need. And if you haven't finalised your **name**, you'll want to do that before messaging as well.

Define your writing style and requirements

Before you start writing, define your style requirements -- tone, voice, style, vocabulary – so that the writing is consistent and match your brand strategy.

Create an elevator pitch

The elevator pitch describes who you are, what you do, who your customers are and why they should buy from you. When you've written it, test it to see how it sounds and how long it takes (not more than 30 seconds).

Create your positioning statements

Write statements of various lengths – 25, 50 and 100 words – so that you have a message length that fits a variety of materials. The shorter statements focus on the value and brand position; the longer ones add features and benefits.

Create a tagline/slogan

Your tagline/slogan is a more succinct phrase used in campaigns. It can be one word or a short phrase and for most business writers, it's harder to create. You may want to hire a copywriter for this one.

Create your mission statement

An average mission statement describes why you're in business. A great mission statement is compelling, shows why you're different and conveys your company's personality.

Determine where to use the messages

Make sure to use your new messages consistently. Train your team to use the messages and audit your materials periodically to make sure they're still working in the future.

What's next?

Your messages feed all of your communications with your market. Use them in your **sales literature and tools**, your **website** and then in all of your **campaigns**.

CHAPTER 11

Sales Literature & Tools

Do you know many companies that can sell their products or services without literature or other supporting materials? It's tough to do so.

Sales literature and tools help you to communicate and strengthen your messages. They're also known as 'marketing communications' or 'collateral' and they may include:

- ❏ Company brochures
- ❏ Product data sheets
- ❏ Case studies
- ❏ White papers
- ❏ Powerpoint presentations
- ❏ Websites
- ❏ Newsletters
- ❏ Reference lists
- ❏ Proposal templates
- ❏ Calculators

The printed word can carry a lot of credibility, so your materials are important tools in your arsenal. They reinforce your brand and can create a lasting impression on your prospects if done well. Plus a single printed piece can reach multiple decision makers when your primary contact passes it along.

Good literature and tools are tightly integrated with your sales process. Rather than inundating a prospect with all of your information at once, break that information into distinct pieces that answer a prospect's key questions at a specific stage in the process. As a result, your prospects can quickly absorb what's most relevant, make decisions more quickly and move to the next stage.

Best Case	Neutral Case	Worst Case
Your sales literature and tools are strong elements in your arsenal. They convey your brand, speak directly to your prospects, and deliver the right amount of information at the right time. They truly help you to move the prospects forward as quickly as possible.	Your literature and tools are typical and general. They convey much of the information your prospects need, but lack the singular focus to be as effective as they could be.	Your literature and tools don't support your brand or value proposition – they're working against you.

Before you begin

Develop your sales tools and literature after you've created your **brand strategy, corporate identity** and **messages**. You may also identify the need for new materials when you write your annual **marketing plan**.

Analyse your current materials

If you think your existing literature and tools could be more effective, take inventory:

- ❏ Review each piece to determine its sole focus.
- ❏ Ask your sales team and others for feedback on whether the piece works.
- ❏ Make sure the piece supports your value proposition and brand strategy.
- ❏ Make sure each piece is delivered at the right time.

Determine what materials you need

List the steps of your sales process and then:

> Brainstorm the materials you could use to answer a prospect's questions at each step
>
> Define a singular purpose for each piece of literature or tool

Write, design & print your materials

To develop your content, focus on the singular purpose of each piece.

> Outline the content that needs to be in each piece
>
> Hire vendors for design and writing if needed
>
> Research and write the content
>
> Develop your design requirements
>
> Design the piece
>
> Get quotes and work with your chosen printer to ensure that you're happy with the final outcome.

What's next?

If you think your **website** could be stronger, it's a logical next step. Like literature, your site should support your sales process, deliver valuable information and reinforce your brand. It can also be used for a wide variety of marketing campaigns.

CHAPTER 12

Websites

These days, most business buyers use the web to read news, research solutions, find vendors and learn about other companies. And whether they learn about your company online or through other means, most buyers and potential partners will review your site before they do business with you.

Your website is potentially the most powerful sales and marketing tool you have. A good site plays an enormous role in your sales process and can help you:

- ❑ Generate leads
- ❑ Nurture existing leads and move them closer to purchase
- ❑ Deliver information about your products and services in a compelling way
- ❑ Process orders, cross and up-sell, and run special promotions
- ❑ Communicate with existing customers and distribution channels
- ❑ Generate publicity

Think of your site as an interactive brochure that speaks with different groups and converts visitors into prospects and customers. It's an extension of your brand and an example of the quality of work you do.

Although a site can be a substantial investment, it doesn't have to be expensive; it just needs to effectively communicate with your market and support your brand. Yet when you develop your site with richer content and some basic marketing functionality, you gain broad and potentially lucrative marketing capabilities.

Best Case	Neutral Case	Worst Case
Your site is more than a brochure; it sells. You use it for a variety of internet marketing campaigns: Search, e-mail, webinars, ongoing communications, publicity and more. Your content is relevant; you know how many leads your campaigns generate and what those leads cost. You can quickly create landing pages for campaigns, thus converting traffic into prospects.	You have a standard site with basic information plus a few press releases and newsletters. You've tried some internet marketing with mixed results. You know your prospects look at your site and it could be better, but it's no different than your competitors. There are bigger priorities than a site redesign, but you suspect that more content and functionality would give you more marketing power.	Your site works against you. It may be the design, content (or lack of), writing, or functionality. It doesn't support your value proposition and you can't do any internet marketing campaigns. You wince when prospects ask for the URL; you know they don't get a good impression from your site and your competitors look better and stronger. You can't quantify whether you've lost any business – but you know you probably have.

Key concepts & steps

Before you begin

Make sure you've tackled your **brand strategy, corporate identity, messages** and **sales literature** before developing your site. A site project may also flow from your annual marketing plan, particularly if you've decided to pursue more aggressive internet marketing campaigns.

Develop your project team and timeline

Work backward from key deadlines to create your project timeline. Give yourself plenty of leeway since website projects can easily hit snags. If you're launching a sophisticated site, make sure you've included all of the relevant departments in your project team.

Define your needs

Before you hire a designer or developer, decide what your site needs to accomplish:

- ❑ Your major goals
- ❑ How the site will support online and traditional marketing campaigns
- ❑ How the site will help you generate leads, nurture prospects, communicate with your market, process orders, etc.
- ❑ The information and functionality you believe you'll need
- ❑ Whether a basic design is fine or whether you'll need something more unique and customised

Develop your content

- ❑ Determine a preliminary game plan for your internet marketing efforts so that your site can support them.
- ❑ List the "users" who will visit your site: new prospects, existing prospects, customers, partners, media, job applicants, vendors, etc.
- ❑ Develop a list of the information and tools (content) each user wants to find on your site.
- ❑ Review competitor and other industry sites for additional ideas.

Organise the content

Organise your content so that the users can quickly find what they need. You'll also incorporate Search Engine Optimisation ("SEO") techniques to help with search engine rankings. For example, your home page is most important to search engines; if you don't have rich content on that page, you won't rank as highly.

Identify functionality you'll need

❑ You may want to display product details and process orders.

❑ Determine whether you want to let customers access their records on the site.

❑ Evaluate other functionalities, such as search, calculators, streaming video or other capabilities.

Develop your design requirements

Like your sales literature, your site should convey your brand. Use your regular colour palette, typefaces and personality traits as much as possible.

Identify any last requirements

❑ Requirements for updating and managing the content

❑ Programming technologies you do and don't want in the site

❑ Reporting requirements

Qualify and hire vendors

Unless you have an in-house web development team, hire vendor(s) for design, writing and/or programming. Review their past work and talk with recent clients to make sure you're comfortable with their strategy and skills.

What's next?

Once you're finished with your building of the site, use it to communicate with your market and generate leads, especially through **e-mail**, **online advertising** and **search marketing.**

However, after constructing your site successfully to your taste and statisfaction, keep **updating** and **developing** your website, as frequently as possible with relevant information abut any new product launched by your company, or any new service provided by your company, etc. These online marketing strategies will definitely add on to and strengthen your customer base.

CHAPTER 13

Customer Relationship Management (CRM)

Customer Relationship Management (CRM) is a term that refers to two things:

- ❏ A company's strategy for managing leads and customer data
- ❏ Software that manages that data

In its simplest form, CRM is a database where sales and marketing teams store critical account data:

- ❏ Contact and account information (contact names, e-mails, phone numbers, SIC codes, addresses, etc.)
- ❏ Source of the lead
- ❏ Sales representatives' names and activity history (calls, e-mails sent, inquiries, etc)
- ❏ Purchase history
- ❏ Projected revenue by customer/customers
- ❏ Marketing campaign data, etc.

CRM can also be an important reporting tool. For example, you can use it to:

- ❏ Generate revenue projections for a product, a sales representative and your company as a whole
- ❏ Tie revenue to the original marketing campaign

- ❑ Pull up lists of leads and activities by sales representatives
- ❑ View the number of leads you have at each step in your sales process
- ❑ Track your progress against your goals
- ❑ Manage marketing campaigns
- ❑ Capture leads from your website
- ❑ Minimise the time your team spends creating manual sales and activity reports

Here are three examples of how different companies can use the CRM:

Enterprise CRM	Mid-Market CRM	Small Company CRM
Company A is a national insurance company that sells directly to consumers and uses a single CRM system. Thousands of sales representatives across the country log in, enter prospect data and use the system to manage their sales activities. At regional and corporate offices, many departments use the data to run real-time reports – revenue projections, sales metrics, customer growth, customer satisfaction, and ROI for marketing campaigns – to effectively manage the business.	Company B's 60 employees use CRM to manage 1200 customer records and thousands of prospects. The system links to the 're-quest information' form on the company's website; leads are intelligently routed directly to the sales representatives for that territory. The CRM links to the company's accounting software. When orders appear in the CRM system, they also appear in the appropriate financial reports. The operations team uses the system to fulfil orders and track shipping and service history.	Company C has four sales representatives, two account managers and a marketing manager. They use a web-based system and pay per user per month. They started with a simple version and upgraded when they needed more functionality. Their system tracks leads by campaign, assigns leads to sales representatives, tracks activity, estimates revenue, launches and measures marketing campaigns, and stores templates for sales letters, e-mails and presentations.

Every company needs to store this information somewhere, and there are CRM products with very simple functionality and complex multimillion-dollar versions. When you use the right CRM system, you gain knowledge and power to keep your team on track and measure progress against goals.

Best Case	Neutral Case	Worst Case
Your CRM matches your marketing, sales, customer service and retention strategies. It's easy to use and provides reports that eliminate the need to generate tedious manual reports. It may integrate with other software like accounting and inventory, enabling your entire team to view important data and reports in a short time.	Your CRM meets your basic needs. Your team uses it fairly consistently, but you have to keep on them to update data regularly. It doesn't have all of the reporting capabilities you'd like, and revenue reporting tends to be manual, so there's some lost sales productivity. It's fine, but it probably isn't the best solution.	You don't have a solid system for managing customer information; it's kept in various files or databases that aren't linked. It's difficult and time-consuming to create revenue projections, sales reports and marketing campaign reports. The result: lost revenue, less productivity and loss of opportunity.

Before you begin

When you build your **competitive positioning** and **brand strategies**, you may decide that you need a system that helps you better manage your customer relationships and information, driving you to look at the CRM. You may also decide to evaluate the CRM after developing **marketing campaigns** or a **marketing plan** that will require better lead capture, reporting and other marketing capabilities.

Once you have a defined **sales process**, you'll enter it in the system so that your representatives can track the steps, each account goes through.

Analyse your needs

If you're new to the CRM, or have a system that could be improved, define what you need.

❑ Decide what information your team should be able to access and how they'll use it.

❑ Identify who needs to use the system and where they're located (i.e., in different offices).

❑ Determine what reports you'll want to generate, particularly your revenue and pipeline reports.

❑ Identify the marketing programs you'd like to be able to run and how that information can help you better manage your accounts.

If you've outgrown your current system, you may be able to purchase add-ins to give your existing system more power. You may also decide to evaluate new systems to give you the true functionality you need.

Evaluate and compare the CRM software

Once you've defined your requirements, look for a CRM package that meets your needs. Remember that many systems come in several versions; you can start with a basic version and upgrade as you grow, but make sure the upgrading process is seamless.

Implement and monitor your system

When you're nearing the end of your selection process, get ready for implementation.

❑ Create an implementation team.

❑ Develop a schedule for key tasks: configuring fields, migrating data, creating reports, training users, etc.

❑ Create a solid training plan.

❑ Launch the software.

❑ Do follow-up training to ensure that your team uses the software as planned. Most implementations fail because employees don't use the software properly.

Gather feedback and modify the software configuration as needed. Always make it as intuitive and powerful as possible.

What's next?

The CRM software can dramatically improve your **sales management**, so make sure that your entire team understands how to effectively use the software to make selling easier.

CHAPTER 14

Sales Management

Good sales management is one of the simplest ways to increase your revenue and profitability.

Sales management is about leading the people and process your company uses to sell prospects and service customers. Responsibilities include:

- ❑ Building the right sales strategy
- ❑ Hiring the right team
- ❑ Creating the right compensation plans, territories and quotas
- ❑ Setting the right projections
- ❑ Motivating your team
- ❑ Tracking revenue against goals
- ❑ Resolving conflicts
- ❑ Training and coaching sales representatives
- ❑ Managing processes
- ❑ Getting the sale!

Why is there a sales management chapter in the Strategic Marketing Process?

Your sales team is the voice of your company. In fact, your representatives may be the only people with direct customer interaction. They may be responsible for prospecting, selling and managing existing customers. They control the dialogues with your market, gather feedback, and deliver on your value proposition and brand promise.

The sales team will make or break your marketing efforts. Even if you're not personally responsible for the sales team, it's important to understand their role and draw on that knowledge to create better marketing programs.

Sales and marketing serve one purpose: to generate revenue. They should be completely aligned in their understanding of customer needs, their messages, and the process they use to identify prospects, sell, close and manage. They should work together as a unit, providing valuable feedback to improve all of their strategies.

When departments aren't aligned, your company wastes time and opportunity. For example, when salespeople rewrite literature and tools to their liking, your messages are diluted and salespeople are doing something other than selling.

Small improvements in your team's skills and processes can often produce substantial results. Even great salespeople can benefit from coaching; if your team is struggling, there's room for improvement. And with the right attention to your pipeline and goals, you can make sure you're on track to hit your numbers and make adjustments as needed.

Best Case	Neutral Case	Worst Case
Your sales team is a revenue machine. They have the right skills and experience; they're motivated to come in each day and close business. You coach them regularly to improve their performance.	There are strong and weak players on the sales team. Some require a lot more hand-holding than you'd like; there isn't always time to give them the help they need. As a result, their close ratios are much lower.	Your sales team isn't strong. They may not have a dedicated sales manager to help improve performance. They may not have enough experience, especially if you're a small company that can't yet afford the big hitters.

Table Contd......

Best Case	Neutral Case	Worst Case
When problems arise, they're dealt with swiftly. The sales team does a great job delivering the company's value proposition, brand strategy and messages.	They're probably not hitting their quotas, but they're not a major liability to the company.	You have a pipeline but don't know what's happening with prospects; it takes longer than it should to close deals. You suspect that you need an entirely new sales operation.

Before you begin

It's always a good time to increase your focus on sales management. Your **sales process** and **CRM** are important tools that can help you manage your team, forecast results and keep your team on course.

Create the right compensation plan and tie it to your revenue goals

Great salespeople want to make money. Tie the plan to your revenue goals and make sure that you're compensating your representatives for the right things. For example, if your representatives don't earn commission for managing 'house' accounts, they'll spend their time going after new businesses and you could lose valuable existing customers.

Set realistic quotas

Be realistic about what a salesperson can accomplish in a set timeframe. Good salespeople can be demotivated by unrealistic quotas, which can lead to turnover.

Hire the right people

To build a great team, start with a strong recruiting effort. Create a detailed job description so you know exactly what you need in your candidates. Cast a wide net, use a thorough interview process, and go after the candidates you really want.

Coach and provide feedback

A good manager actively works with the sales team. Train your representatives thoroughly and coach them to improve their skills. Go on calls, establish performance measurements, and provide feedback. If a representative has trouble in a particular area, create an action plan and measure the improvement.

Generate good reports

You'll need good sales reports to measure team and individual progress. Yet you don't want your sales representatives to spend valuable sales time creating manual lists and reports. Instead, develop automated

CRM system. With good reports, you can see problems much earlier and take actions more quickly.

Motivate!

them to read, attend seminars, network, and keep refining their skills.

What's next?

Keep working with your team, improving their skills, and adjusting as needed. Hire the right people, manage them well, and enjoy their success!

CHAPTER 15

Business Development

Organisations apply the term, 'business development' (a.k.a. 'biz dev.') to a variety of activities.

'Business development' in the Strategic Marketing Process refers to high-level partnerships that generate revenue, create better products and/or increase efficiency. These partnerships can help you:

- ❑ Access new markets
- ❑ Increase sales to the existing markets
- ❑ Improve your access to technology
- ❑ Boost your productivity
- ❑ Gain capital (human or financial)

In a true partnership, companies collaborate to achieve a common goal. It's more than a short-term promotion, such as a special offer or marketing to each other's customers. Instead, **it's an agreement to do business together while sharing responsibilities, resources, risks and rewards.** For example, here are three examples of true partnerships:

To Create New Products	To Increase Efficiency	To Create New Products
A computer manufacturer enters a partnership with a fashion designer	A software company has a fantastic new product, but is inundated with customer	A design firm partners with a direct mail fulfillment firm to offer each other's

Table Contd......

To Create New Products	To Increase Efficiency	To Create New Products
to create a limited-edition laptop and matching case. They create a team of employees from both companies to design and market the product. The computer manufacturer produces the computers, the designer creates the bag, and they share revenue fairly based on their cost structure.	service calls, they can't handle. They approach a telemarketing firm that specialises in the software industry. Instead of just hiring the telemarketing firm, they create a partnership. The telemarketing firm provides service for a greatly reduced fee, then receives a substantial commission for selling the software company's other related software. The partners work closely together to maximise their revenue on the sales program.	services to their respective clients. Each company promotes the partnership to new prospects & existing customers. They offer the service with a single point of contact – if a design client needs mail services, the design firm manages the implementation rather than just referring the client to the mail firm. Each company bills the other at special rates so there's room for a fair markup, providing each company with additional revenue.

In these examples, each company has distinct responsibilities in the partnership. They each devote resources (either time or money) to the program, and if it fails, they have similar levels of risk. They've also fairly divided the rewards.

The first step in a successful partnership is structure; the right arrangement aligns both companies towards an important common goal. The second step is execution; A partnership should be managed like any business with careful attention to details, solid communication and focus on the end goals.

With the right structure and management, your business development deals have the greatest potential for success.

Best Case	Neutral Case	Worst Case
The partnership is balanced and productive for both parties. You share responsibilities, resources, risks and rewards, and the partnership delivers substantial revenue, cost savings or new opportunities for both the companies.	Your partnership isn't balanced -- perhaps you have more responsibilities and resources allocated, or you don't share fairly in the rewards. It produces value, though not what you had expected; you hope the situation will improve with time.	You enter into a partnership and invest substantial resources, but the partnership goes awry. Your 'partner' isn't delivering as needed and you don't have much recourse – your partner isn't really providing resources or sharing risks. As a result, you end the partnership and lose valuable time and money on the deal.

Since these partnerships involve multiple departments in each company, there are usually a number of people involved in the deal. It's often an executive or high-level 'biz dev' person leading the process for each company, although in small companies a sales or marketing executive will take the reins. However, creating a partnership is more complex than pure sales -- it requires a solid understanding of the business and operational objectives of multiple organisations.

Before you begin

You can think about business development at any time. It's common to identify potential partnerships during annual planning time, so many companies start pursuing deals after finishing a new **marketing plan**.

Identify potential partnership

Brainstorm to identify partnerships that can help you meet your goals. For example, there may be related companies with customer relationships in a different market; you may have vendors or suppliers who can help you improve your products or firms that can help you round out your services.

would provide, how the partnership would be managed and what each party would invest and earn.

Identify the right 'biz dev' person to lead the project

A good 'biz dev' person has a broad understanding of business strategies and operations, and he can also negotiate and close a complex sale. It's a different skill set than many sales representatives offer, but you may have a representative or executive on your team who can do these kinds of deals -- or you may tackle it yourself.

Pitch a partnership

Develop a strong pitch to capture the attention of your potential partners; focus on the high-level benefits for each party. As you move through the sales process, cover all aspects of the partnership including detailed structure and terms.

Share responsibilities, resources, risks and rewards

You have a much stronger chance of success when a partnership is balanced. As you negotiate the deal, make sure your interests are completely aligned and that each party is contributing in all areas.

What's next?

When you set up a partnership, make sure your company manages and executes so that you'll reap the full benefits. As part of the partnership, you may launch new marketing

marketing program.

CHAPTER 16

Customer Retention

How much have you invested in sales and marketing over the last few years? Thousands? Tens of thousands? Millions? Tens of millions?

Customer retention is about keeping the customers you've spent that money to acquire. And if you're in an industry, where they make multiple purchases over the years, your entire team should be very focussed on retaining those customers:

- ❑ Delivering service that's consistent with your value proposition and brand
- ❑ Cross-selling, up-selling and asking for referrals from existing customers
- ❑ Developing programs to increase customer loyalty and decrease turnover
- ❑ Knowing the lifetime value for different segments and using that data to improve your marketing
- ❑ Prioritising retention as a major focus in your annual marketing plan

Studies say it costs ten times more to generate a new customer than to maintain an existing one. If you have a small number of customers, losing a few could cripple your company. Even if you have a large number of customers, a small increase in your retention rate should dramatically increase your profits. In fact, in his book, *The Loyalty Effect*, Fred Reichheld writes that "A five percent improvement in customer retention rates will yield between a 25 to 100 percent increase in profits across a wide range of industries."

With strong retention marketing, it's much easier to grow your revenue and profitability. Do you see your company in any of these scenarios?

Best Case	Neutral Case	Worst Case
Your company is focussed on customer retention and it has paid off. Renewals are high; you put a lot of effort into campaigns and service for existing customers. Sales representatives are incented to keep customers happy. You use financial modelling and surveys to identify problems and focus on vulnerable customers. Your revenue has grown substantially each year because you're adding new customers without losing the current ones.	You know how important it is to retain customers. The representatives who service the existing businesses are good, but you've lost some customers that you shouldn't have. You've done surveys but haven't done anything major as a result. And you struggle with the commission for current business – some people argue that you shouldn't pay at all because they're house accounts. As a result, you have to replace the current customers each year.	You don't formally market to your current customers. You know your service could be better, but you haven't had the time to develop an improvement plan. You definitely have more turnover than you'd like. As a result, you're continually investing to generate new customers. Your revenue profit margins are much lower than they could be, and the churning takes its toll on your organisation.

Before you begin

You can work on your customer retention strategy at any time, and **marketing campaigns** may be an important part of your strategy. You may also decide to increase your focus on retention when you're writing your annual **marketing**

plan. But if you're losing customers, don't hesitate to focus your energy on retention right now.

Determine your retention strategy

Your value proposition and brand strategy should drive your retention plan. For example, if your value proposition is customer intimacy, your customers are counting on great service. If they're buying on price, you'll usually focus more on automating service to minimise costs.

Build your team

❑ In some industries, the original sales representative is the best person to manage an existing client -- for example, the account may require ongoing selling. In other cases, it's better to transition the customer to an account representative, who focusses on a day-to-day management.

❑ Once you've decided how to structure the team, determine how many people you'll need and start recruiting.

Pay commission for renewals and growing the business

Your current customers are your most valuable assets; if your sales representatives don't earn commission on renewals, they'll be incented to spend their time chasing new businesses instead.

Market to existing customers

Put as much effort into your current customer campaigns as you do the rest of your marketing programs. Know your audience, grab their attention, focus on the offer and measure your results. Use campaigns to:

❑ Nurture your customer relationships
❑ Encourage them to buy again

Expand your relationships by cross-selling, up-selling and asking for referrals

Identify customers who are at the risk of defecting

Continually deliver on your value proposition and brand promise

Measure purchase intent and loyalty, not 'satisfaction'

Customer feedback can help you improve your products and continue your relationship. However, it's not effective to measure 'customer satisfaction' because it's so vague. 'Satisfied' doesn't mean they intend to keep buying. Instead, focus on the behaviour: Ask whether they intend to buy again and why or why not. Ask what three things you can improve and whether they'll provide referrals. These questions provide more actionable insight than 'satisfaction.'

Treat a survey as a marketing campaign. Give your customers a reason to respond, thank them and share the results.

Use data to evaluate large groups of customers

If you don't have personal relationships with your customers, use data to identify customers, who haven't purchased in the normal timeframe. They may be at risk of defecting and you can launch retention campaigns encouraging them to stay.

What's next?

Refine and improve your customer retention strategy and execution -- they may deliver the highest Return on Investment (ROI) of all your marketing programs.

CHAPTER 17

Telemarketing

The phrase, 'cold calling' sends chills down the spines of many businesspeople. It's often viewed as an intimidating, difficult and boring process ... and that means it doesn't get done as often as it should.

Telemarketing campaigns help companies reach a group of targeted prospects or customers to communicate a message, gather feedback, and determine a next step for the relationship. Telemarketing can be an important part of any marketing strategy – for example, you can use it to:

- ❑ Generate leads
- ❑ Qualify prospects, who have downloaded information from your website or attended a webinar
- ❑ Follow up on a direct mail or e-mail offer
- ❑ Take orders for special promotions
- ❑ Keep your marketing database current
- ❑ Conduct marketing research

In many companies, sales representatives should make hundreds or thousands of cold calls every month to set appointments and/or generate leads. But busy representatives usually prefer to work on closing their existing pipeline. Prospecting often slips on the priority list; as a result, the sales pipeline isn't always filled with new prospects.

If cold calling is an effective way to introduce your company to new prospects, don't ignore it. Instead of forcing a sales team to devote time to prospecting, many companies use an in-house or outsourced telemarketing group to make a high volume of calls, find decision makers and qualify leads for the field sales group.

When telemarketers handle prospecting, salespeople can spend 100 percent of their time selling and closing. Your company can produce more revenue in the same amount of time; your representatives earn more commission, they're doing what they love, and they're more satisfied with their jobs.

You can use a telemarketing team in a variety of campaigns:

Outbound Lead Generation	Outbound Campaign Support	Inbound Sales Support
Company A's telemarketers call targeted lists. They identify the decision-maker, ask qualifying questions, and gauge the prospect's needs and interest level. If a prospect meets certain criteria, the telemarketer sets a follow-up appointment for a sales representative.	Company B increases their response rates by including phone calls in campaigns. For example, when they hold an event at a trade show, they call prospects before mailing an invite to lift their response rate. They also follow up with those who don't respond.	Company C makes sure that prospects who visit their website can call and speak with someone immediately. They use an inbound sales support team to answer questions and probe callers. The representatives send follow-up materials and a field sales representative follows-up with the most qualified prospects.

With the right strategy and proper management, a good telemarketing operation can produce great value for your company.

Best Case	Neutral Case	Worst Case
You have a team or vendor to prequalify leads and handle inbound and outbound calls for marketing campaigns. Your team succesfully represents your brand to your market. You have strong management in place and can easily report on key statistics: contacts per hour, statistics by representatives, etc. You set goals and hit them consistently.	You have a vendor or in-house team and their performance is average. If they're in-house, you have some statistics, but not enough, and there's a fair amount of turnover in the position. In fact, you're always training someone new. You see the value in using telemarketing and you think your operation could improve.	You don't have a telemarketing operation. Sales representatives make their own cold-calls but they simply don't make enough. When prospects call from your website, there frequently isn't a person available to talk with them live. And when you need to include a phone call in a marketing campaign, it's an enormous battle to get representatives to make calls.

Before you begin

If you can immediately gain new prospects and customers, don't hesitate to launch a telemarketing campaign right now. You may also decide to pursue telemarketing after developing your annual **marketing plan**.

Set your goals

You can use telemarketing in many ways; brainstorm the campaigns that will work best for your company. For example, you may need to generate leads for your sales team or use telemarketing to support other marketing campaigns.

Forecast and budget; determine whether to build in-house or outsource

❏ Estimate your call volume, then think about hours of operation, fluctuations in call volume, and the skill set you'll need in your representatives.

- ❏ Your call volume also drives your headcount, software, phone system and the office space you'll need.
- ❏ These requirements will help you decide whether to use a vendor or hire and manage a team in-house.
- ❏ If you look at vendors, the requirements will make your discussions easier and faster.
- ❏ Budget for everything including headcount, software licenses, bonuses and management.

Develop good scripts

Representatives will need to capture attention, build value, and close a good script which will help them in their work.

- ❏ Make your scripts conversational, simple and focussed on the end goal.
- ❏ It helps to make and listen to calls as you're developing and refining your script. What looks good on paper may not work on the phone.
- ❏ Get feedback from your team as well.

Train and coach your team

- ❏ Regular coaching and quality assurance is crucial.
- ❏ Engage your representatives, role-play and guide them through calls.
- ❏ Listen to calls regularly, evaluate your representatives and coach them to improve their performance.

Make it fun!

- ❏ Telemarketing is a tough job and turnover is a big issue.
- ❏ Make things fun with contests, events and other incentives.
- ❏ Make their space comfortable and interesting – tiny cubes, old chairs and windowless rooms don't put a smile in anyone's voice.

Report your results

Define the reports you'll need -- your system may not be able to provide all of the data, but you can probably find an alternate solution.

Use reports to consistently evaluate progress and improve your campaigns.

What's next?

It's all about execution, so manage your team and devote the resources necessary for success. Telemarketing can be very effective and is often underutilised in Business to Business (B2B) marketing plans.

CHAPTER 18

Trade Shows & Events

There's an old saying in business that people buy from people. If that's the case, it's a good idea to get people together as often as possible!

Trade shows and events are gatherings for businesspeople with common interests to achieve a goal. The B2B companies use these events to generate leads, nurture prospects, build awareness, conduct training, or enhance relationships with existing customers. Options include:

❑ **Trade shows:** You can exhibit during the exhibition, sponsor round table discussions or speeches, advertise in show materials and/or host your own reception at the event hotel or a restaurant in town.

❑ **Seminars or conferences:** Sponsor an industry conference or create a seminar and market it to your prospects.

❑ **Networking meetings:** Participate in and/or sponsor industry or local meetings; you can also create a one-time or ongoing breakfast or lunch meeting series for your prospects to attend.

❑ **Webinars:** Webinars are online seminars with slides and audio; you can use them to generate leads and communicate with large groups at a lower cost than a live meeting.

❑ **Events for the arts, sports or charities:** You can participate in these events as a sponsor with advertising,
blocks of tickets, promotions and a reception for your
Very Important Persons (VIPs).

Many shows and events are major investments with a lot of
logistics:

❑ Event planning
❑ Travel
❑ Shipping
❑ Set-up
❑ Promotion
❑ Sales materials
❑ Sales follow-up
❑ Measurement

When executed properly, a great event could produce a
large percentage of the leads a company needs to generate
over an entire year. With a halfhearted strategy, companies
usually get lackluster results.

Best Case	Neutral Case	Worst Case
You use trade shows, special events and/or webinars to generate new prospects and reach out to existing prospects and customers. You stand out from your competitors, deliver compelling information and create meaningful dialogues with your market. You set goals and	You regularly attend trade shows and you've tried a few webinars with mixed results --there's a lot of competition for your prospects' attention. At shows, your team does a decent job of qualifying leads and following up; you know you generate new business but you don't know how	You exhibit at trade shows and you're never satisfied with your leads. It's hard to stand around for days and you know leads fall through the cracks in the weeks afterward. Your competitors are always doing something big at the shows but you haven't been able to afford anything, but your booth.

Table Contd......

Best Case	Neutral Case	Worst Case
measure them, and you know your ROI is worth the investment. You also implement marketing programs to drive traffic and continue dialogues after the event so that leads don't fall through the cracks.	much. It seems like you could be generating a lot more business from these programs, but you're not sure how to do it.	You haven't tried any other events because they're an enormous effort for very little payoff. You've never really been able to measure the results from the shows you attend – you get a handful of leads and that seems to be it.

With a solid strategy, plan, investment and measurement, events can be an exciting marketing tool to the B2B marketers.

Before you begin

Most trade shows and events take careful planning with many details to address. It's best to create your trade show and event strategy months in advance. Better yet, outline your events in your **marketing plan** so that you can build your pre-event and post-event campaigns effectively.

Choose an event that matches your need

❑ Define your marketing objectives: generate leads, nurture the existing leads, build relationships, train and educate, or raise visibility/brand awareness.

❑ Focus on the type of events that can and will help you meet your goals: Industry events and shows, networking events, seminars and conferences, sponsored events, charity events, webinars, etc.

❑ Brainstorm to create a list of events and themes that will fit with your goals.

Outline your event strategy

Understand what your prospects need and how you can deliver it during the event. For example, think about the content your prospects want and how you should structure the event.

Create your event plan

- ❑ Once you have a strategy, start the planning process: time, date, location, theme, event flow, materials, script, responsibilities and more.
- ❑ Plan for sales-related activities: what happens with new leads, how you'll prioritise leads, follow-up timing, materials they should receive, etc.

Promote your event

- ❑ To drive attendance or participation, develop a thorough promotional campaign with a strong call-to- action.
- ❑ Use multiple media to touch your market frequently and consistently.
- ❑ If you're sponsoring another company's event, be sure to promote your participation – don't leave it up to someone else to drive your traffic.

Script your event and execute

- ❑ A good event script and plan will help you execute without problems. Create a detailed timeline; rehearse appropriate activities with your team; make sure everyone clearly understands their responsibilities.

Measure your event's success

Look at your goals-to-actual and share the results with your team.

Document everything you learnt so that you can use that information next time.

What's next?

Trade shows and events typically generate new relationships or foster the existing ones. It's important to set solid follow-up procedures with your sales team so that valuable leads don't fall through the cracks.

Trade shows and events are increasingly being used by countries and companies to market and showcase their products as global competition for market shares intensifies.

CHAPTER 19

E-mail Marketing

E-mail marketing has been a boon for consumer marketers since the mid-90s. A few years later, B2B marketers discovered its value, and e-mail campaigns have become an important tool for businesses in all stages and industries.

E-mail marketing enables you to cost-effectively communicate with your market in a way that's immediate and relevant. With e-mail, you can:

❑ Nurture leads
❑ Build brand awareness
❑ Obtain prospects
❑ Build customer loyalty
❑ Generate sales

You can usually launch a campaign and measure your results fairly quickly, making e-mail a great option for time-sensitive programs. It's easy and inexpensive to test different aspects of your campaign on a segment of your list, so you can hone your creativity and your offer to generate the best possible results.

Here are three sample e-mail campaigns:

Generate New Leads	Direct Sales	Build Brand Awareness
Buy or rent a list and send a short, compelling message to generate interest in your product. Drive prospects to a special page on your website to download a white paper, a demo or other offer. Capture basic information and follow up via phone several days later.	Buy or rent a subscriber list or send the campaign to your current prospects and customers; compel them to click to your website to read, learn and buy.	Use e-mail to keep in touch with prospects and customers. Deliver timely, valuable information that makes them want to read your messages. Add news about your company, special offers, etc., but focus on content and information rather than pure sales.

E-mail is more editorial than advertising, and it's powerful because it can support and even drive a sales process. Yet like any medium, it has its challenges. Businesspeople get hundreds of e-mails (or more) each day, so you'll need to get your message past spam filters and give them a reason to read. You'll also need a strong offer, valuable editorial content, appropriate design and a good fulfilment and measurement process.

You can reach a wide audience with e-mail, but that doesn't mean you should. It's most effective when you really target so that you can speak to specific needs. Think of it as a one-to-one communication – personalised, relevant, timely – not a blast.

If you've used e-mail in the past, do you see your company in one of these scenarios?

Best Case	Neutral Case	Worst Case
You have a strong e-mail program with very specific goals.	You are generally satisfied with the results. You send announcements	You use e-mail as a quick-fix – when you're low on leads,

Table Contd......

Best Case	Neutral Case	Worst Case
You use technology to deliver your messages effectively. Your campaigns offer strong content and messages; you create custom landing pages to convert clicks to prospects. You continually test your designs, copy, list and offer to improve your response. As a result, you usually meet your ROI and business goals.	about products and offers; you occasionally use e-mail to generate leads or keep your name in front of the existing ones. You occasionally test a campaign before launch, but it isn't a major priority. You know your campaigns could be stronger, but you haven't had time to learn more.	you do a blast message; if you haven't reached out to customers, you create a quick newsletter. You generally don't target your prospects – you blast one message to your entire list. You don't test your campaigns, and you don't know how many of your messages are actually delivered.

Before you begin

Use e-mail to meet the goals you set in your annual **marketing plan**; you can also use them as part of a broader **marketing campaign**. You'll also need to make sure your **website** is strong enough to support your campaign.

Develop your campaign around specific goals

Take the time to strategise and plan your campaign:

- ❑ Develop a tangible objective – for example, to generate a specific number of leads, demo requests, meetings, or purchases.
- ❑ Profile and target your audience. You can reach a large audience through e-mail, but that doesn't mean you should – narrow targeting, i.e., you avoid speaking directly to them.
- ❑ Create a good offer and compelling call-to-action, and present it early in your message – readers skim.
- ❑ Plan a series of e-mails to create an ongoing campaign – it takes multiple touches to generate response.

❑ Don't forget fulfilment – if your prospects expect a phone call or e-mail, deliver it quickly or you could lose their interest.

Invest in good content

Few people want to read e-mails that look and feel like ads. Instead, offer information that's relevant to your recipients. It's an investment to develop that content, but it's the content that gets people to open your messages and continue to read them over time.

Choose the right technology

If you've never launched an e-mail campaign, you'll probably need to use an E-mail Service Provider (ESP), typically a web-based service. Choose a reputable ESP to help you stay compliant with spam legislation and get your messages to your prospects' inboxes – a major issue in e-mail marketing. A good ESP can raise your delivery rate, manage your opt-in and opt-out processes, keep your e-mail list clean and provide reports that can help you improve your results.

Be respectful and follow industry practices

❑ Make sure you're following accepted industry practices – you'll improve your probability of success.

❑ Mail to your house list regularly – even corporate e-mails change rapidly. The more time between campaigns, the higher your rate of bad addresses – and those 'bounces' could trigger spam alerts.

❑ Make sure your recipients can easily opt-out of future communications.

❑ If you're buying or renting a list, make sure it's an 'opt-in' list.

Continually test, refine and improve

It's always wise to test before launching a campaign. If you're working with a new ESP or list, evaluate your delivery and response rate before you roll out. Keep testing and improving your subject lines, headlines and copy, design, offer, landing pages, even the delivery timing. You'll improve all your campaigns in the process.

What's next?

As e-mail becomes more important in your overall strategy, keep learning about the subject and improving your marketing campaigns.

CHAPTER 20

Search Marketing

What's 'search marketing' and why is everyone talking about it?

Search marketing is about gaining visibility on search engines when users search for terms that relate to your business. For most companies, ranking highly in search results isn't luck – it's a result of solid effort in one or both categories of search marketing:

Organic search: When you enter a keyword or phrase into a search engine like Google or Yahoo!, the organic results are displayed in the main body of the page.

When your prospects search for information about your products and services, you want to rank highly in search engine results. By 'optimising' your site, you can improve your ranking for important search terms and phrases ('keywords'). You can also improve your rank by getting other important sites to link to yours.

Paid search enables you to buy listings in the 'sponsored' area of a search engine. There are a variety of *paid search programs*, but the most common is called Pay-Per-Click (PPC), meaning you only pay for a listing when a prospect clicks your ad.

In search marketing, companies focus on driving more traffic to targeted areas of their websites. They use search to:

❑ Generate new leads

❑ Sell products

❑ Build their brand/brands

❑ Divert traffic from their competitors

Studies show that most businesspeople research their problems, potential purchases and vendors online and use a search engine in the process. And the higher the price of the product/service, the earlier they search.

For many businesses, generating only a handful of additional serious prospects can make a substantial difference in revenue. Using search marketing may efficiently produce these additional prospects.

Best Case	Neutral Case	Worst Case
You're generating very targeted prospects through your search marketing programs. Your site is optimised and you've built a lot of important incoming links, so you rank well in organic results for targeted searches. You use paid search to supplement that traffic and you create custom landing pages for your campaigns to convert visitors into prospects.	You've built a new website and it's been optimised for search, but you don't rank in the top 10 for anything but your company name. You've tried some paid search with good success; your conversion rates on the traffic are okay but could be better. You know that search marketing is a solid opportunity – you're just figuring out how to improve your results.	Your website isn't optimised for search and you're nowhere to be found on search engines, even for very targeted terms. In fact, you may not even rank for searches on your company name. Unfortunately, your competitors show up on the first and second pages for the terms your prospects use. As a result, your competitors are winning new businesses and furthering their lead/leads in the market.

Before you begin

Depending on your search strategy, you may need to make major or minor improvements in your **website**.

Create your search strategy

Look at your short and long-term goals to choose whether to focus on organic or paid search (or both). It takes time to improve your organic search rankings, but you can launch a paid search campaign tomorrow. However, there are other considerations: the amount of traffic you need, your budget, and your marketing objectives. Once you've reviewed the pros and cons, you can select the search strategy that's right for you.

Generate a list of keywords

Before you can optimise your site or launch a paid campaign, generate a list of keywords – terms your prospects use when looking for information you can deliver. You can brainstorm, copy keywords from competitors, or use online tools to generate a list and traffic estimates.

Optimise your website

❑ Rewrite your content so that it's rich with the keywords you've chosen.

❑ Make sure the content is organised in the best possible manner.

❑ Eliminate any technologies that prevent search engines from reading your content (for example, search engines can't read Graphics or Flash content).

❑ Register your site in important directories that play a vital role in search engine results.

Generate inbound links

❑ Search engines reward you when sites link to your site – they assume that your site must be valuable and you'll rank higher in search results. The higher the 'rank', of the sites that link to you, the more they count in your own ranking. Your aim should be to get linked with popular industry authorities, recognised directories, and reputable companies and organisations.

Implement additional internet campaigns

These programs can improve your search results:

Creating Really Simple Syndication (RSS) feeds to distribute updated content from your site to other websites

Including a blog on your site

Distributing search-optimised press releases on the web

Start testing paid search

To begin using paid search, you'll:

Develop targeted landing pages for each campaign

Write your ad(s)

Create an account with a search network that's important to business users (i.e., Google)

Set up your campaign with the network

Start tracking your results

What's next?

Focus on converting your new prospects into customers, and then keep the cycle going.

CHAPTER 21

Online Advertising

Internet marketing isn't just for consumer marketers or large B2B firms – it's a powerful vehicle for companies of all sizes.

Online advertising offers B2B marketers an opportunity to reach very broad or very targeted prospects to generate leads, communicate a message and raise visibility. In the Strategic Marketing Process, the term, 'online advertising' refers to three general types of campaigns:

- ❑ Banner ad campaigns on B2B websites
- ❑ Ads or sponsored content on targeted e-mail newsletters
- ❑ Affiliate programs that enable other companies to put your ads on their sites in return for commission on clicks or sales

While a B2B marketer has a smaller universe of prospects than a consumer marketer, the value of each prospect is typically far greater. With a targeted campaign and a good offer, you may only need to generate a handful of highly qualified prospects to generate substantial revenue.

Here are three different online ad campaigns:

Generate New Leads	Direct Sales	Increase Your Visibility
Promote a white paper, webinar or demo that can help prospects who are in the early phases of their research. Drive them to a special landing page; provide details about the offer and capture key pieces of data so that you can follow up when the prospect is ready.	Run ads to sell a particular product or service. Drive prospects to a special landing page that describes your offer in detail; if you need to provide additional information, create supplemental pages as needed. Really focus on converting those prospects into sales.	Run a campaign to share a message, promote an event or offer, or raise awareness about your products. Your goal is twofold: Drive click-throughs and generate awareness. Use landing pages designed to convert a visitor into a prospect or customer.

What are the benefits of online advertising?

- ❑ **Timing:** Reach businesspeople when they're actively looking for information, vendors and solutions.

- ❑ **Immediacy:** You can test and launch very quickly and generate response almost immediately.

- ❑ **Targeting:** You can deliver your message to very specific audiences.

- ❑ **Lead generation and nurturing:** You can capture prospects early, provide valuable information, and nurture them throughout the sales process.

- ❑ **Cost:** You can reach a large audience quickly and at a lower cost than many other media.

- ❑ **Scalability:** You can run campaigns of any size at any budget level.

- ❑ As with any marketing program, it's important to develop a good strategy, target your audience, test, measure and improve – especially because it's easy and inexpensive to test different aspects of your campaigns to generate the best possible results.

Best Case	Neutral Case	Worst Case
Your online ad campaigns are a strong element in your marketing mix. You use them to generate prospects and customers, but gaining visibility is also important. You calculate the Return On Investment (ROI) so you can compare the return of these investments versus your other programs. You continually test your ads and landing pages to maximise your response rates.	You run campaigns periodically and they're moderately successful. Prices are high, but you reach a targeted audience. You occasionally test and tweak your ads, but it isn't a priority. Since you use cost per click to measure success, you can't accurately calculate the ROI, but you're satisfied with what you're paying for traffic. You think you can generate even more traffic, but without better metrics, you can't divert more funds to these campaigns.	You've advertised on a few sites and generated some traffic, but you don't have data to indicate whether your campaigns are successful beyond initial visits. You don't create special landing pages – you drive visitors to your home page, and you rarely test your ads. You cringe at the prices for the sites you'd really like to use, and you think you're wasting money since you're paying for impressions not clicks.

Before you begin

Before you launch an online campaign, it's important to have a good website that can measure your traffic and convert visitors to prospects or customers. It's also helpful to address your online campaigns in your annual **marketing plan and budget**.

Develop a tangible goal

For example, determine how many click-throughs or leads you need to generate, then estimate your response rates to figure out how many impressions you'll need. Make sure you know how you'll measure your campaign as well.

Target your audience

Profile and target your audience. You can reach a large audience with your ad, but that doesn't mean you should their needs.

Create a good offer and compelling call-to-action

Your ad needs to generate interest and get people to click

a benefit. Keep your message simple and clear.

Focus on conversion

When you run a great ad, continue the message and momentum on your website. Don't drive prospects to your home page; instead, create unique landing pages that focus on the topic you used to generate their interest. Focus and sell!

Continually test, refine and improve

It's easy and inexpensive to test your online campaigns. You can test the offer, the design of your ad, the size and location of the ad, or the sites you choose. Start with the element

two versions of the ad. Then run them against each other to see which performs the best.

When you keep testing in this way, you can greatly increase

increase in the number of qualified leads and new customers you generate.

What's next?

Keep refining your online campaigns and your website to drive and convert traffic.

CHAPTER 22

Publicity

Have you ever read a story about a company and then contacted them to learn more about their product or service? Or perhaps, you've heard a Chief Executive Officers' (CEO's) speech and found yourself researching the company later on?

Publicity in the media can be extremely valuable in building credibility and awareness for your company. For example, a legitimate news story is an endorsement that can reach a wide audience for very little cost beyond your own creativity and time. There are many forms of publicity including:

- ❏ News stories/interviews in trade journals, industry sites, newspapers, magazines, etc.
- ❏ 'Expert' quotes in a story written by a journalist or a blogger
- ❏ Self-authored stories published on websites or in industry publications
- ❏ Speaking engagements

Publicity is a highly cost-effective strategy that can:

- ❏ Build awareness about your products/services, expertise and people
- ❏ Drive prospects to your website

❑ Drive participation in a promotion or event

❑ Educate the market about problems your company can solve

❑ Create an ongoing dialogue with the market

The key to success: Create newsworthy stories. They should be interesting, relevant, timely, and offer new information or insight to your prospects.

Even if you don't think you have newsworthy content to share with the world, you can benefit by implementing small programs to raise your visibility. At the very least, you should include news releases on your website and home page; they help in search engine rankings and enable prospects to see what you've been doing. Publicity isn't about luck. It's about investing in a good Public Relation (PR) program, and it can really pay off over time.

Best Case	Neutral Case	Worst Case
Your company is very well-known in your industry. When you launch a product or have a newsworthy story, important publications write about you, and you're often quoted in industry articles. You capitalise on the role the internet plays in publicity -- your press releases drive prospects and customers to your website. You also use blogs or other online publicity techniques to create a strong presence on the internet.	You use a PR sporadically with mixed results – an occasional blurb in an industry journal, a miscellaneous quote as an expert. You put press releases on your website and distribute them online; you know they make your site more interesting to prospects, but you're not sure whether you're gaining the full benefit from your efforts.	You don't use any form of PR. You may be a startup or an established company, but you're not known by your industry press. You see your competitors featured in industry publications even when your solution may be better; your company doesn't seem to have that level of credibility, and you're not sure how to get it.

Before you begin

Tie your publicity strategy to goals you've identified in your annual **marketing plan**.

Create a publicity strategy

Don't just 'shotgun' press releases when you need to drum up some attention. Plan your publicity strategy as you would any marketing campaign:

- ❑ Develop a calendar that ties story ideas to key events and spreads your storytelling out over the year.
- ❑ List events that may offer good speaking opportunities.
- ❑ Identify publications, reporters and bloggers who cover subjects that are relevant for your company.
- ❑ Create traditional and online press materials to give reporters support materials for their stories.
- ❑ Know the audience for each story and carefully target your media.

Develop newsworthy story ideas

Every day, journalists are bombarded with press releases touting new product releases, business alliances, research discoveries, etc. But journalists don't just make announcements -- they need to tell compelling stories that their readers will find interesting and useful. A trade journal may run one-paragraph blurbs about new products, but to get headlines, photos, interviews and pages, you need to develop real stories.

Like movies, good news stories are often about conflict. An endless stream of positive information is boring. Instead, develop stories with substance: Good vs. Evil, Nature vs. Nurture, Race Against Time, Company A vs. Company B, Employee Against the World, Company vs. the System.

In addition, good stories can be extremely 'viral' when you distribute them on the web.

Market your stories and expertise

Journalists need stories; when you have a story, you have something to offer. With a quick, courteous phone call and a simple pitch, you may get a journalist to say, "Yes, I'm interested in that story, send me your material." That three-minute phone call could potentially make a substantial difference in your campaign success.

Reach out when you identify a potential speaking engagement or find a journalist or blogger who may want to quote an expert from your company. Be sure to prepare a short pitch and support materials as well.

Use the internet

Many PR experts say the traditional press release is dead. These days, a worthwhile PR strategy has to capitalise on the internet.

Write a second version of your normal releases with rich keywords and a format that helps search engines find the release.

should be an actual page on the site, not a PDF.

Send your release to internet news distribution services.

updated content to other publishers.

What's next?

It's difficult to measure the return on publicity, but if you're really focussed on creating stories and reaching out a wider auidience, you have strong potential for success. One big story or important speaking engagement could generate fantastic results, so keep working at it!

CHAPTER 23

Direct Mail

For many years, direct mail has been an important marketing vehicle. Even though many companies have turned to e-mail and internet marketing, a targeted and well-produced mail campaign can still be highly effective.

Direct mail campaigns can generate leads, promote special offers, support other campaigns, communicate with customers and raise your visibility in your market. You can be very simple or wildly creative depending on your goals – for example, you can use:

❑ A handwritten note

❑ A simple but effective sales letter

❑ A postcard with a four-colour image on one side and a printed message on the back

❑ A digitally-printed brochure with the prospect's name printed in the headline and the body copy

❑ A custom piece that you develop for a specific purpose

Direct mail can be an efficient vehicle for your company if you focus on strategic, targeted mailings instead of large bulk mail campaigns, which draw very low response rates at much higher costs than online marketing. Instead, consider using mail for small campaigns:

❑ Invite current customers and top prospects to an event you're holding at a trade show

❑ Send product literature with the prospect's name and custom specifications printed into the brochure itself (via digital printing)

❑ Announce a compelling sale

Here are three sample mail campaigns:

Generate New Leads	Nurture Existing Leads	Cross-Sell Current Customers
Mail a personalised, hand-signed letter to targeted prospects. Quickly introduce your value proposition; invite prospects to call or visit your website to view a demo, download a special report, or request a quote. Follow up with a phone call a week later.	Mail a quarterly 'industry update' or case study with graphs and reference info – more than you'd be able to provide in an e-mail newsletter. Focus the piece on a typical objection, prospects have before they buy.	Develop a piece that delivers a compelling case for your current customers to buy related products and services. Include a strong call- to-action; encourage customers to call or visit your website to learn more and buy.

In B2B, it's better to think about mail as an integral part of a larger campaign. Don't just mail and wait for the phone to ring. Instead, plan a campaign that starts with an introduction via mail, then perhaps a follow up phone call from a sales representative and a demo delivered via e-mail.

When you use the right strategy and execution, direct mail can be a strong addition to your marketing arsenal.

Best Case	Neutral Case	Worst Case
You're happy with the ROI on your mail campaigns. You design each piece to grab attention, convey a simple message and move the prospect towards action. You test your mailings and tweak the headlines, envelopes or offers to increase response, and you use targeted and current lists.	You've had some success with mail campaigns. Sometimes they're spur-of-the moment; you know you could do a better job of planning ahead and focussing your message. You typically use mail in conjunction with a phone call. You don't really test your campaigns and try to improve results, but your response rates are acceptable.	You've used mail but feel it was a waste of money. The list was expensive and didn't necessarily have the right contact names. The mail piece and postage was expensive and contained a lot of information, yet it didn't generate the response you planned. You had counted on it generating a lot of leads that you ended up having to find elsewhere.

Before you begin

Make sure your direct mail campaign is tied to the goals you've set out in your **marketing plan. Define your goals.** Tie your campaign to a specific objective – for example, the number of responses you need or the number of customers you want to generate. Then design your campaign to meet your specific goal.

Target your audience

Narrow your audience as much as you can – you'll be able to speak more directly to your prospects with better results. You'll also save on postage and production.

Focus on the offer

Don't overwhelm your audience with every detail about your product and company. Focus on the offer itself – the purpose for the mailing, the call-to-action. For example, if you're promoting a software demo, explain what the demo will help them learn and why they should request it now. Touch on the key benefits, but don't muddy your message by including every detail about the software and the history of your company.

Develop your content, then your creative

First determine how much copy you'll need, what kind of graphics or photography you'll include, how to promote the offer, etc. Once you've defined the content, you'll need to achieve your goals, then start the design process. If you're working with a design and/or writing team, explain your requirements in a 'creative brief' so you're all on the same page.

Tackle the campaign logistics

Make sure you plan how your piece will be folded, stuffed, addressed, stamped, mailed, etc. If you're running large campaigns, you may want to hire a vendor to handle this step.

Test, measure and continually improve

set of records from your list, send your mailing, measure your response, then tweak the mailing and send it to another subset. You can improve the list targeting, your offer, the envelope design, the copy and the design itself. Commit to continuous improvement and use what you learn in all future campaigns.

What's next?

Measure your ROI and compare it against your ROI for other media. Mail can be a substantial investment and it should produce a return that is as great as or better than your other media.

CHAPTER 24

Traditional Media

Marketers have used traditional media such as print, radio, TV, yellow pages and even outdoor ads to reach consumer markets for the last 50 to 100 years.

Traditional media can also play a role in the marketing mix for many B2B companies. These media often reach a broad audience and thus can be relatively expensive. Yet in your industry or region, they may be very effective in helping you reach your market. For example:

In many industries, print ads in monthly trade journals are an important vehicle to reach decision makers.

If your company sells to a certain geographic region, directory listings and ads may be crucial for reaching buyers when they're searching for solutions.

You may need to reach a wide variety of prospects in different industries, so you may advertise in a regional or national business publication, newspaper or radio program.

You can use these media to generate leads, build visibility, share your message and/or drive specific promotions. They're especially helpful when you use them in conjunction with other media in a larger campaign.

Here are two sample campaigns that incorporate traditional media:

Use Print & Online To Generate Leads	Use Radio To Generate Leads & Awareness
To generate leads, you run a print ad in an industry journal and a banner on the publication's website and monthly subscriber e-mail. The prospect calls to take advantage of your offer or visits a unique landing page on your website, then fills out a form. A sales representative calls and sets up an in-person presentation.	You run a schedule of about 30 ads on a talk radio show that reaches a broad base of businesspeople in your industry or region. As part of your package, you buy exclusive sponsorship of the show. You receive special mentions throughout the show, and you use the entire campaign to drive traffic to a specific landing page on your website. The page continues your message, captures the prospect's information or encourages a phone call. Your telemarketing team qualifies leads and transfers hot prospects to your sales team.

It's important to treat these programs as longer-term investments because responses tend to come in gradually -- they aren't as immediate or measurable as internet marketing, telemarketing or direct mail. Targeting may be an issue and you may not be able to measure the branding impact of your campaign, but they're solid vehicles when they're in line with your goals or used in a larger campaign.

Best Case	Neutral Case	Worst Case
You understand the strengths and limitations of traditional media, and you use them effectively in campaigns to drive awareness and response. You test your campaigns to improve over time and you measure the campaigns to the best of your ability. While you don't measure the	You run a sprinkling of traditional media campaigns and track the number of calls they generate. You know they work to some degree, but you can't quantify the results that well. The ads themselves are about average but you rarely test them to improve. You know it's important to be in	You don't evaluate your buyers very carefully; you don't have specific goals and thus can't measure whether you're successful or not. You don't really test your ads either – they offer a lot of information and you can't really say whether they work either for branding or direct response.

Table Contd.....

Best Case	Neutral Case	Worst Case
value of your brand-building, you do adjust your ROI calculations to incorporate an allowance for that value.	the vehicles you choose, and you stick with the same tactics because your competitors are doing the same thing.	You're wasting your budget and time on programs that could be vastly improved.

Before you begin

Make sure your campaigns are tied to the goals in your marketing plan.

Develop a strong strategy

First, determine what you need to accomplish. For example, you may need to generate a specific number of leads, raise your visibility in a certain industry or geography, or communicate a key message across different media. Set tangible goals for your media plan.

Each media has benefits and drawbacks. When you've defined your goals, you can decide which vehicle will work best. Make sure you know how to measure your campaign as well.

Decide whether to buy media in-house or through an agency

Media buying can be a tricky and time-consuming process. If you have a lot of media to buy, you may want to hire an agency. You'll pay for their services, but they may also have more buying power to negotiate better deals and find ways to reach your target market more cost-effectively.

Consider targeting when comparing costs

Media sales representatives may quote you a flat rate for a particular ad or they may quote a cost per thousand (CPM) impressions. You may pay a higher CPM for a more targeted media than a general one, but if you calculate your cost per targeted impression instead, you can truly compare apples to apples.

Create a compelling ad and call-to-action

creative, but keep your message simple and clear. Include a call-to-action: Encourage prospects to call or visit a special landing page to learn more about a particular offer or program.

Continually test, refine and improve

It's wise to test any campaign before spending your entire budget. If you're considering multiple publications, run the same ad in two different ones to see which generates the best response. Or test different headlines and offers. Your goal is to find the ads and publications that generate the best response, then run them for the remainder of your campaign.

What's next?

Keep testing and refining your campaigns so that they deliver on your goals.

CHAPTER 25

Recruiting

What's the difference between a great company that outperforms the market and an average company? Great products, services, strategies and execution ... and your employees are responsible for those successes. A company can accomplish far more with a strong team in place than it can with an average team.

Recruiting is essential for building a strong sales and marketing function. And like marketing, recruiting is both an art and a science:

Art: Getting to know a candidate to understand whether he or she is the best fit for the job.

Science: Defining detailed job requirements so that you can search for the right candidates; conducting a wide search; using a process for moving candidates through the process; measuring results.

It's time-consuming to recruit marketers, sales representatives, telemarketers and account managers. Yet these positions are the heart of your success, so give your recruiting efforts the time they deserve.

Best Case	Neutral Case	Worst Case
You have a strong team with the skill	You create job descriptions before you	In the worst case, you have team members

Table Contd......

Best Case	Neutral Case	Worst Case
sets you need for success. Before each hire, you develop a solid job description, compensation plan and profile, so you're sure about the qualifications and personality type for the position. You screen and interview your candidates efficiently and when you hire someone, he's or she's excited about the job. You have little turnover and your employees are truly a valuable asset to the company.	recruit and you usually get an acceptable number of resumes. Sometimes the process drags out longer than it should, and you've made some offers to candidates that weren't a great fit. You do have some average performers on your team, but there are no major issues.	who aren't qualified for their roles. They require a great deal of management and you're concerned about the time it takes to replace them. It's difficult to find qualified candidates, especially because experience is expensive. Morale isn't great and people view their jobs as tedious – there isn't a lot of excitement and positive energy in your team.

Before you begin

You may need to recruit to meet a variety of goals: grow your sales team, hire a business development executive, create an account management team, build a telemarketing operation, or add resources to another area of your company. Strive to recruit the best employees for all areas of your business at all times.

Define the position

- ❏ Evaluate the job responsibilities; prioritise the skills and experience your candidates will need.
- ❏ Develop specific criteria you'll use to evaluate your candidates.
- ❏ **Write a compelling ad:** A good ad inspires qualified candidates to apply for the position. It needs to stand out among the ads they'll be reviewing, and it needs to convey credibility, your brand and message.
- ❏ Think of your ad as a sales pitch to a prospect and write it carefully with your applicant in mind.

Cast a wide net

❑ Referrals are a great source for qualified candidates. Encourage everyone in your company to contact vendors, customers, friends and family about open positions. Create a job description they can pass around.

❑ Advertise in appropriate publications and websites. If you're concerned about cost, measure your cost per applicant and per hire, then use the best-performing sources the next time around.

❑ If you're not finding qualified candidates, keep investing ... don't settle for mediocre applicants just because you don't want to spend more money looking for the right person.

❑ If you're doing a lot of hiring, make sure to post open jobs on your website and include content that speaks to the applicants. Good candidates will look at your site to learn about the company.

Follow your process

❑ Create a process and follow it: Resume review, phone screen, interview, maybe a second interview, reference check, offer. A good process saves time -- for example, don't invite a candidate for live interviews if you haven't done a good phone screen; you may find that they're not a good fit during the phone call.

❑ Respect the time and talent of all your candidates. Thank them for interviewing and let them know when you've extended an offer to someone else. You never know when you'll cross paths again.

What's next?

After you bring aboard new marketing and sales employees, make sure they understand your competitive positioning, brand strategy and messaging, so that they can deliver on those strategies every day.

Also keep a record of their daily, weekly on monthly performances so that it becomes easier for you to evaluate their output. They should give manually or mail their daily or weekly work reports. Give them sales targets and set incentives for them that will motivate them to work harder and achieve their individual targets.

CHAPTER 26

Vendor Selection

Have you ever had a difficult time hiring a vendor? Even with years of experience in a particular area, it can be a time-consuming process. It's even more difficult if you're hiring a vendor for a function you don't know very well.

Vendor selection is an important part of the marketing process because few companies have the resources to complete every project in-house. For example, you may need a vendor's expertise and resources to:

- ❑ Write, design or produce sales literature, ads or other creative materials.
- ❑ Design, write or develop your website or online campaigns.
- ❑ Run a telemarketing campaign.
- ❑ Develop your media plans and buy media.
- ❑ Provide e-mail or search marketing services.
- ❑ Manage the print and fulfilment process for a mail campaign.
- ❑ Handle publicity.
- ❑ Write messages and slogans.

There are many benefits of outsourcing; you can gain deep industry experience, access new technologies, or save money. Thanks to the efficiencies a vendor can provide.

But it's important to carefully evaluate and manage your vendors to reap those rewards.

Do you see your company in any of these scenarios?

Best Case	Neutral Case	Worst Case
Your vendor delivers great results on time and on a fair budget. The vendor is easy to work with and enables you to focus on other things, making you more productive. A great vendor relationship can truly enhance your business.	Your vendor delivers acceptable results at the price you expect. You probably need to keep on top of the vendors to make sure deadlines are met, and you devote time to properly manage the relationship.	Your vendor provides poor work, is over-priced, doesn't meet important deadlines, and/or is difficult to work with. In the worst case, you lose time and money trying to manage the vendor; you may have to fire the vendor and start from scratch.

Before you begin

Next time you need a vendor for one of your projects, use this process to find, evaluate and select the best person or company for the job.

Define your needs and timeline

If possible, determine what you're looking for before you start your search. You may want to set an initial budget, then develop a timeline for your search, especially if you have important dates to hit.

Identify and analyse vendors

Use the web and ask for referrals to find a list of qualified vendors. Develop a list of qualifying questions and narrow the field to a handful of companies.

Create your Request for Proposal (RFP)

If you're looking for very simple, straightforward services, you can ask bidders to provide a proposal and quote. For more complex or intangible projects, it's better to create a Request for Proposal (RFP) that asks bidders to respond to very specific questions in a consistent fashion. A standard RFP is particularly helpful when:

> The vendor is providing a comprehensive service.
>
> The project is intangible or has many elements, such as a website.
>
> You have very specific evaluation criteria and need to compare 'apples to apples'.
>
> You're evaluating a large number of bidders (more than four).

Evaluate, negotiate and award project

> Rate your bidders on the important criteria and narrow the field.
>
> Negotiate pricing and terms with your finalists, but remember the adage, "You get what you pay for."
>
> that best meets your criteria for success.

What's next?

Continue to improve your vendor research, RFPs, and vendor management. Most companies use a variety of vendors over time, and good vendor selection and management will help you improve results.

CHAPTER 27

Return on Investment (ROI)

Marketing campaigns are investments. And like any smart investment, they need to be measured, monitored and compared to other investments to ensure you're spending your money wisely.

Return on investment (ROI) is a measure of the profit earned from each investment. Like the 'return' you earn on your portfolio or bank account, it's calculated as a percentage. In simple terms, the calculation is **(Profit – Investment) Investment**.

ROI calculations for marketing campaigns can be complex. You may have many variables on both the profit side and the investment (cost) side. But understanding the formula is essential if you need to produce the best possible results with your marketing investments.

With solid ROI calculations, you can focus on campaigns that deliver the greatest return. For example, if one campaign generates a 15% ROI and the other 50%, where will you invest your marketing budget next time? And if your entire marketing budget only returns 6% and the stock market returns 12%, your company can earn more profit by investing in the stock market.

ROI helps you improve your ongoing campaigns. When you tweak your offer or launch a campaign to a different list, you can compare the ROI and focus on the version with the best performance.

Finally, ROI helps you justify marketing investments. In tough times, companies often slash their marketing budgets – a dangerous move since marketing is an investment to produce revenue. By focussing on ROI, you can help your company move away from the idea that marketing is a fluffy expense that can be cut when times get tough.

Best Case	Neutral Case	Worst Case
You measure and track the ROI of all of your marketing investments. Your campaigns deliver the highest possible returns and you're able to improve them over time. Your organisation understands and agrees with the choices you make because there's solid data to support your investments.	You calculate the ROI on some investments, but because it can get complex, you don't attempt to measure it at all times. You have a general idea of how your Investments perform relative to each other, but you can't pinpoint the exact return you're generating. And in tough times, your budget is Cut.	You don't measure the performance of any of your investments. In fact, marketing is viewed as a cost, not an investment at all. Your company isn't sure what works and what doesn't, and it's a struggle to meet the goals.

Before you begin

It's a good idea to measure the ROI on all of your marketing investments – after all, you're in business to earn profits. If your sales process is long and complex, you may choose to modify or simplify your ROI calculations, but a simple calculation is more useful than none at all.

Confirm your formulae

There are several figures you'll need for your ROI calculations:

❑ Cost of Goods Sold (COGS): The cost to physically produce a product or service.

❑ Marketing investment: Typically you'd include just the cost of the media, not production costs or time invested by certain employees; however, in certain cases, it may be better to include all of those figures.

❑ Revenue: It can be tricky to tie revenue to a particular campaign, especially when you run a variety of campaigns and have a long sales process. Your finance team may have some suggestions for estimating this figure.

❑ Companies calculate these figures differently, so confirm the formulae your company uses – your finance team or accountant can guide you.

Establish an ROI threshold

Set an ROI goal for your entire budget and individual campaigns; set a floor as well. By doing so, you gain more power over your budget. If you project that a campaign won't hit the threshold, don't run it; if you can't get an ongoing campaign over the threshold, cut it and put your money elsewhere.

Set your marketing budget

When you have an ROI goal and annual revenue/profit goals, you can calculate the amount of money you should spend on marketing – just solve the ROI formula for the 'investment' figure. You'll be more confident that you're spending the right amount of money to meet your goals.

Calculate ROI on campaigns; track and improve your results

❑ Tracking the ROI can get difficult with complex marketing campaigns, but with a commitment and good reporting processes, you can build solid measurements, even if you have to use some estimates in the process.

❑ Use your ROI calculations to continually improve your campaigns; test new ways to raise your ROI and spend your money on the campaigns that produce the greatest return for your company.

What's next?

The more you understand the ROI, the more power you have over your investments. Continue to learn, improve your reporting capabilities and use your ROI to improve your sales campaigns and generate more profits for your company.

CHAPTER 28

Customer Lifetime Value (CLV)

Do you know what an average customer is truly worth to your company? By calculating your Customer Lifetime Value (CLV), you'll be able to answer that question.

The CLV is the amount of profit a customer delivers to your company for as long as the customer is buying from you. It's typically calculated as the net present value (the value in today's dollars) of the profit you'll earn from all of a customer's purchases over time. When you know your CLV, you have an extremely powerful tool that helps with:

❑ **Acquisition:** You'll have a better understanding of what you can spend to acquire customers.

❑ **Targeting:** You'll know which customer segment delivers the most profit to your company, and you can focus more marketing efforts towards that segment.

❑ **Return on investment (ROI):** By using CLV in your ROI calculations for marketing campaigns, you'll have a much more accurate measure of campaign performance.

❑ **Customer retention:** You can determine how much you can spend to profitably retain customers.

❑ **Single-customer profitability:** You can calculate the profitability of an individual customer.

The CLV becomes more important as your marketing budget rises and your customer base grows. Yet even an early- Stage Company can benefit with a simple CLV estimate.

Best Case	Neutral Case	Worst Case
You know how much an average customer in each of your segments is worth to you. You focus your acquisition efforts on your most valuable segments, and you know how much you can spend to profitably retain your customers.	You have an idea of who your most valuable customers are, but you're not really sure how much you should spend to acquire or retain them. Your ROI measurements for your marketing campaigns are probably very general, though still helpful.	You don't know how much a customer is worth or how much you should spend on acquisition or retention. You're not sure what your marketing budget should be, and you're not confident about the quality and quantity of the investments you're making.

Before you begin

You'll want to look at the CLV for different groups of customers, so make sure you've defined those segments. The CLV is a valuable tool to improve your marketing campaigns and budget; it's also used when you're working on customer retention and the ROI.

Confirm your formulae

There are several figures you'll need for your CLV calculations:

- ❑ Cost of goods sold (COGS): The cost to physically produce a product or service
- ❑ Gross profit: The difference between the price of your product and the COGS
- ❑ Companies calculate these figures differently, so your first step is to confirm the formulae your company uses.

Determine your customer segments

The CLV calculation is most valuable when you measure it by customer segment – similar groups of customers who use your products/services in a similar way.

For each segment, determine how long an average customer stays with you -- the 'lifetime'

Look at your customers' buying patterns and calculate the total number of purchases they make including the time between those purchases.

Calculate your CLV for each segment

❑ Once you know the average lifetime, you'll calculate the total profit you earn on all of their purchases

❑ The probability that they'll make successive purchases

❑ The value of future revenue if you had the cash today

Use CLV to improve your acquisition and retention marketing

Once you have a CLV for each customer segment, you can

❑ Set a maximum budget to acquire a particular type of customer.

❑ Calculate whether a particular deal will be profitable.

❑ Look at current customers who haven't purchased according to the pattern you estimated in the calculation. They're more likely to defect, so launch a retention campaign to those customers.

❑ Plug it into your ROI projections. It's more accurate to calculate your return on a campaign when you use the total profit the customer represents over time, not just the profit you earn on the first sale.

What's next?

Keep applying the CLV and using it in your marketing strategies and plans. When you use the CLV and the ROI in all of your sales campaigns, you have powerful tools to help you grow your company's revenue and profit.

The Customer Lifetime Value (CLV) is particularly relevant to all those companies who sell directly to consumers or who are distributors.

CHAPTER 29

Copywriting & Graphic Design

You've probably seen quite a few marketing materials, such as brochures, websites and ads that are dull, uninspiring, and worst of all, confusing.

Good copywriting and graphic design create powerful communications with your market. They help a creative vision and message that resonate with your audience. Good copywriting and graphic design will:

- ❑ Reinforce your value proposition
- ❑ Evoke your brand
- ❑ Convey your messages in a meaningful, memorable way
- ❑ Improve response and ROI for your campaign

Writers and designers can have broad or very focussed skill sets. For example, a writer may specialise in web copy, technical writing, advertising copy or sales letters. Graphic designers may focus on web design, logos, flash design for online campaigns or print design. Agencies may offer a variety of services, but they can also be just as specialised.

When you create literature or other creative projects, you're making a substantial investment. By using the right people and managing your project effectively, you'll maximise your chance for success.

Best Case	Neutral Case	Worst Case
Your copy and design are powerful; they communicate your objectives simply and in a memorable way. Your prospects 'get it' quickly and are eager to learn more, creating more opportunities for your company.	Your copy and design are average. They may be wordy or not that exiting, but they're not substantially different than what your competitors create. They accomplish what they need to, but could be better.	Naturally the worst case scenario is that your copy is poorly written and your design unappealing. These materials give a negative impression of your company and your prospects choose your competitors over you.

You'll need your brand strategy and messages for any creative project. If you're creating sales literature, you'll need to understand how it fits with your sales process; if the project is part of a marketing campaign, make sure you've finished your strategy and goals so that the literature can support them.

Create a project timeline

Provide a reasonable amount of time between each step so as to each team member can deliver on schedule. The earlier you get started, the better are your results.

Determine what content will be in the piece/ literature

The content should drive the design, not the reverse. If you start with design and try to fill in content later, the piece may not be nearly as effective. Identify the copy, graphics, photos or charts you'll need in your piece before starting the design process.

Use a creative brief

A creative brief is an overview for a project. It can be simple or lengthy depending on the complexity of the project and the amount of background information your team needs. A good creative brief defines:

Deadlines

Goals including the action you want the recipients to take after seeing the piece

Audience

Content

Background information about the product, service, audience, company, etc.

Branding requirements including the desired colour palette, logo usage, fonts, etc.

Establish criteria for the designs

It's much easier to evaluate design concepts when you have specific criteria to measure against. Establish that criteria upfront so that your design team understands what they need to deliver, then use that criteria to choose concepts and provide feedback.

Pay attention to proofs and the press check

Make sure you have a very thorough review process in

and embarrassing error. Also, conduct a thorough press check so that your printed materials completely match your requirements and vision because you wouldn't want your brochure printed on the wrong paper or your colours to be mismatched.

What's next?

Keep looking for good copywriters and graphic designers. With a good team of resources, you'll have someone to call for, no matter what type of project you dream up. Moreover, good copywriters and graphic designers can help you to create innovative and the right kind of ads, brochures or pamphlet designs, you are aiming at.

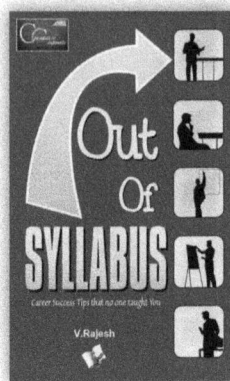

Author: Dr. Nivedita Ganguli
Format: Paperback
Language: English
Pages: 108
Price: ₹ 96.00

Do you feel that life sometimes pulls you down? Do you keep on searching for some light to pull you out of darkness? Do you feel so wrapped up in your own issues that you miss out the real treasure of life? Probably this book may create a full-stop to your search. The episodes present in the book would enable you to see life from a brighter perspective. The 'In a Nutshell' portion following each episode would give direction towards Life Management. Quotations present in form of 'Food for Thought' would give rich nutrition to your thought process. Our wrong perspective towards everyday issues makes life more complicated. Changing perspective would enable us to live life fully.

Author: Anchit Barnwal
Format: Paperback
Language: English
Pages: 168
Price: ₹ 200.00

Just as a winning podium can accommodate anyone on it, each one of us is capable to be a winner, irrespective of our shortcomings and differences. Winners' Podium – Everyone Fits on it, attempts to do just that: make out a winner amongst each one of us.

This book offers elaborate guidelines for a balanced, successful and happy living. It tells how one can find his talent, attract ideas and be successful, both personally and professionally. It also talks of happiness and the steps to it.

Through stories, anecdotes, quotations, examples and day to day observations, this book can inspire you to not only attain that most desirable success, but also to hold on and grow both internally and externally with it.

Author: V. Rajesh
Format: Paperback
Language: English
Pages: 104
Price: ₹ 120.00

It is easy to skip a question during an exam if it is "Out of Syllabus" but what do you do if you are faced with a situation in life for which you were not given any inputs? Can you run away from the situation using the "Out of Syllabus" excuse?

Career is one area where one is expected to know and manage situations. After all a person is paid a salary to be able to handle things and deliver results. The reality is that most people get a lot of academic and conceptual inputs relating to one's career choice but very little practical inputs on how to effectively use the academic learning.

BUSINESS QUIZ BOOK

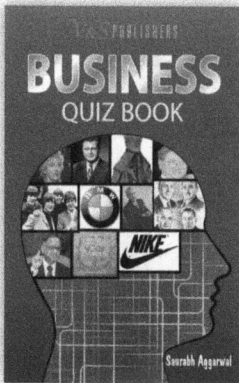

Author: Saurabh Aggrwal
Format: Paperback
Language: English
Pages: 256
Price: ₹ 200.00

Did you know that crossword puzzles first appeared in the New York World in 1913, and soon became a popular feature in newspapers or that Kellog's as a brand had spent $90,000 on advertising, more than 100 years ago in 1906, including one $4000 a page ad in the July issue of the Ladies Home Journal, Apple had lured John Sculley away from Pepsi because they wanted him to apply his marketing skills to the personal computer market. Find facts and trivia from the world of business that will amaze and delight you. The questions in this book have been framed in a way that they are: guessable with intelligent, lateral, or lucky thinking; interesting, amusing, or surprising;

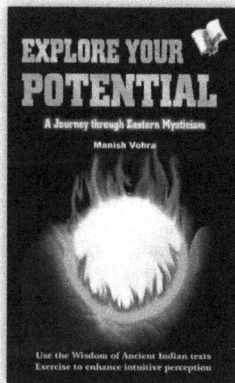

EXPLORE YOUR POTENTIAL
A Journey through Eastern Mysticism
Manish Vohra

Use the Wisdom of Ancient Indian texts
Exercise to enhance intuitive perception

Author: Manish Vohra
Format: Paperback
Language: English
Pages: 128
Price: ₹ 150.00

The book helps the reader to get access to wisdom of several scriptures in one piece. Several sutras which are normally only passed on in the oral tradition are documented in the book.

Just like a magician never reveals his secrets, psychics also never reveal their secrets. There are several books written by psychics but they never reveal their methods. This book not only reveals the methods but also contains several simple exercises to enhance intuitive perception.

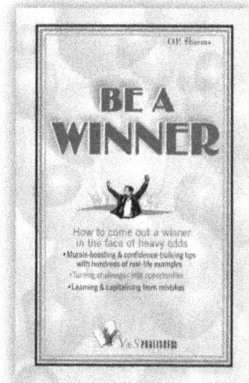

BE A WINNER

How to come out a winner in the face of heavy odds
• Morale-boosting & confidence-building tips with hundreds of real-life examples
• Turning challenges into opportunities
• Learning & capitalising from mistakes

Author: O.P. Sharma
Format: Paperback
Language: English
Pages: 144
Price: ₹ 110.00

Life is full of ups and downs. While we exhilarate in the 'ups', we are totally at a loss when it comes to dealing with the 'downs'. This book has been specifically designed to help you turn the tide in your favour in the face of odds. "Each day is a fresh day — look at it with hope and enthusiasm, yesterday is over." Whatever the situation, you can make the best of things by the right approach.

If you wish to rise in your career, begin liking your work. If you wish to excel, have a healthy approach to criticism. If you want to scare away failures, preserve your peace of mind in the face of heavy odds. If you desire a happy married life, learn to respect your spouse.

How To Become a Successful Speaker & Presenter

Author: Surendra Dogra 'Nirdosh'
Format: Paperback
Language: English
Pages: 112
Price: ₹ 108.00

Have you ever thought of addressing an audience and making them listen to you without batting an eyelid? Do you want to create a trance-like spell on people listening to your speech?

It has carefully dissected every aspect of public speaking and presents a clear map that any aspiring speaker can follow. Besides, it also incorporates the necessary techniques to motivate, captivate, and persuade the audience while making various presentations, etc.

You will master 'How to'

- Conquer stage fright
- Organize material in a flowing manner
- Customise speech for different sets of gathering
- Inspire audience

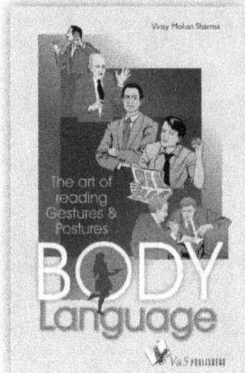

Body Language

Author: Vinay Mohan Sharma
Format: Paperback
Language: English
Pages: 120
Price: ₹ 108.00

Communication is not always through sound or language. Much can be said with gestures or movement of eyes. In fact, more often than not, the Body Language says more than words.

Now discover all the finer points and nuances of body language in this masterly work:

- How thumb gesture displays dominance, superiority and aggression
- How dilation of eyes sends romantic signal
- How a sideways glance indicates either hostility or interest

---

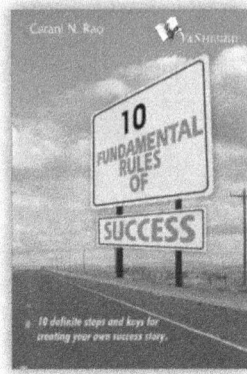

10 Fundamental Rules of Success

Author: Carani N. Rao
Format: Paperback
Language: English
Pages: 124
Price: ₹ 96.00

The purpose of this book is to share with the readers the 10 fundamental rules to achieve success compiled from the vast ocean of literature on success. Some of these essential rules include – setting a goal, positive attitude and self confidence, purposeful desire, planning and preparation, resources, inputs, discipline, action, persistence or perseverance, prayer and values.

Here success is first defined; then the basic rules involved in achieving success are enumerated and explained with relevant anecdotes and stories. Besides these 10 fundamental rules, a set of success formulae as well as virtue capsules have also been added in the book.

---

visit our online bookstore: **www.vspublishers.com**

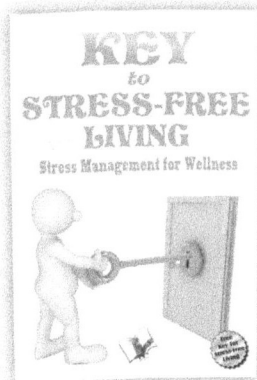

Author: Dr. Jyotsna Codaty
Format: Paperback
Language: English
Pages: 136
Price: ₹ 150.00

There are three primary aspects of life that contribute to promoting unhealthy stress which ultimately kills — inability to make decisions, feeling lack of control in life, and not having a plan or process in place to get to where you need to go. Spread over 18 chapters, this book has put together all the necessary materials to take control of your life, make wise decisions, and be proactive in taking care of things that typically stress you out. This book contains principles and ideas that will go a long way in reducing the stress that people have in this 21st century.

Don't exert extra stress trying to absorb the whole book at one go. Just take one idea at a time, and begin with the next one you think you most need.

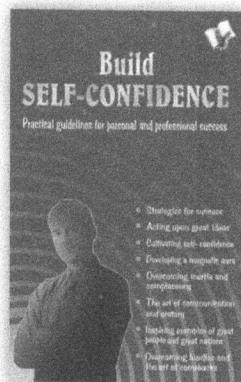

Author: Alankrita
Format: Paperback
Language: English
Pages: 120
Price: ₹ 96.00

Life is never a bed of roses. However, if we know how to negotiate our way between the thorns and hurdles of life, the roses of success will be ours for selective picking. The greatest asset in the quest for success and happiness is our measure of self-confidence. More than half of all life's battles are won or lost in the mind. Therefore, a person needs to saturate his or her mind with positive thoughts at all times.

The book is liberally sprinkled with myriad stories, anecdotes and events that inspire us to follow in the footsteps of those who achieved greatness. It teaches you how to overcome old habits and encumbrances on your journey to the highest peaks and how to mould your circumstances, rather than be moulded by them.

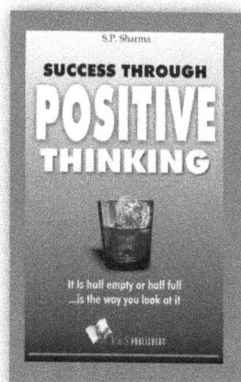

Author: S.P. Sharma
Format: Paperback
Language: English
Pages: 176
Price: ₹ 135.00

The author of this book, S.P. Sharma, not only discusses the problems faced by modern man in this book, but also explains certain religious truths in a comprehensive manner in non-technical language.

It contains useful information designed to help one relieve from anxiety and disturbing thoughts — providing a clear vision leading to a happier life.

It would help one:
• Combat the shocks of life
• Know that nothing is more useful than the awakened self
• Understand the principles that make life happier

It is a wonderful work for anyone who desires to get Success Through Positive Thinking.

www.ingramcontent.com/pod-product-compliance
Lightning Source LLC
Chambersburg PA
CBHW050534270326
41926CB00015B/3216